"Nina Hanssen and Are Høidal have written a unique book about the well recognized and highly successful Norwegian correctional services. Unlike almost any other such institution worldwide the Norwegians have managed to implement workable solutions in this field, resulting in positive outcomes otherwise unheard of globally. They have proven that it actually works to try to correct criminals – rather than just punishing them. The book covers perspectives from both inmates and employees and it will be able to motivate both leaders and employees in the field as well as anybody else who is interested in correctional services. I can highly recommend this very interesting and relevant book".

Frans Ørsted Andersen, *Associate Professor,*
Aarhus University, Denmark

THE NORWEGIAN PRISON SYSTEM

This book presents a comprehensive overview of the Norwegian Correctional Service and the values and principles underlying its operations, using the renowned Halden Prison as a case study. Since its opening in 2010, Halden has been recognized for its uniquely humane treatment of inmates and emphasis on rehabilitation. This book chronicles the lessons learned from the operation of Halden Prison and scrutinizes the effectiveness of its policies.

Staff at Halden operate under a notion of "dynamic security," in which guards circulate around the prison interacting and developing relationships with inmates rather than surveying from a fixed location. Recounted from the perspectives of various actors in the system, and incorporating commentary from international correctional experts, this book sheds light on the effects of the approaches and paradigm shifts that have made Halden different from other prisons. The book presents a balanced picture of how such an approach works, with practical examples of successes and failures.

This book contextualizes how and why this example of reform achieved successful outcomes when others failed, and how it can be improved upon in the future. Illuminating new directions for prison reform, it is essential reading for academics and students engaged in the study of criminology, corrections, and penology, as well as practitioners, administrators, judges, policymakers, and advocates.

Are Høidal has worked in the Norwegian Correctional Services for 37 years. He has held various senior positions over the years at all levels in the service, including 11 years as governor of Oslo prison and now governor of Halden prison since 2009. Are Høidal is a graduate in law from the University of Oslo in 1987.

When taking on the challenge of establishing Halden prison, Mr. Høidal used his competence and values to build a correctional organization where rehabilitation within a safe and secure environment was the main focus. Together with a dedicated staff, Mr. Høidal has established Halden prison as a beacon in the correctional community, achieving a substantial and continuous interest and respect from a wide range of stakeholders from governments, public service, academics, media and NGOs from around the world.

Mr. Høidal is widely used as a speaker and lecturer in the global community of correctional service. He has held presentations at numerous seminars, forums, expert meetings, and universities around the world and is deeply motivated to share his vision and goal of a humane and effective treatment of inmates. With his 37 years from the practitioner field, he speaks with great credibility about how to combine safety and rehabilitation in the best possible way.

Nina Hanssen has 37 years of experience of media and communication in Norway and Kenya. She is a motivational speaker, author, journalist and a marathon runner.

Ms Hanssen has published seven books and is a member of International Positive Psychology Association (IPPA). Her interest is positive psychology and flow. She is a motivational speaker in Talerlisten.no and, since 2015, the national leader of APF – the oldest trade union for journalists and editors in Norway. She currently works as a reporter in LO Media.

THE NORWEGIAN PRISON SYSTEM

Halden Prison and Beyond

Are Høidal
Nina Hanssen

Cover image: © Shutterstock

First published 2023
by Routledge
605 Third Avenue, New York, NY 10158

and by Routledge
4 Park Square, Milton Park, Abingdon, Oxon, OX14 4RN

Routledge is an imprint of the Taylor & Francis Group, an informa business

© 2023 Are Høidal & Nina Hanssen

The right of Are Høidal & Nina Hanssen to be identified as authors of this work has been asserted in accordance with sections 77 and 78 of the Copyright, Designs and Patents Act 1988.

All rights reserved. No part of this book may be reprinted or reproduced or utilised in any form or by any electronic, mechanical, or other means, now known or hereafter invented, including photocopying and recording, or in any information storage or retrieval system, without permission in writing from the publishers.

Trademark notice: Product or corporate names may be trademarks or registered trademarks, and are used only for identification and explanation without intent to infringe.

Library of Congress Cataloging-in-Publication Data
Names: Høidal, Are, author. | Hanssen, Nina, author.
Title: The Norwegian prison system: Halden Prison and beyond/Are Høidal, Nina Hanssen.
Description: New York, NY: Routledge, 2023. | Includes bibliographical references and index.
Identifiers: LCCN 2022030615 (print) | LCCN 2022030616 (ebook) |
  ISBN 9781032050782 (hardback) | ISBN 9781032050775 (paperback) |
  ISBN 9781003195887 (ebook)
Subjects: LCSH: Halden fengsel (Halden, Norway) | Prisons–Norway. |
  Corrections–Norway. | Prisoners–Norway–Social conditions. |
  Prisoners–Rehabilitation–Norway.
Classification: LCC HV9735.H352 H3546 2023 (print) | LCC HV9735.H352 (ebook) |
  DDC 365/.94822–dc23/eng/20220712
LC record available at https://lccn.loc.gov/2022030615
LC ebook record available at https://lccn.loc.gov/2022030616

ISBN: 978-1-032-05078-2 (hbk)
ISBN: 978-1-032-05077-5 (pbk)
ISBN: 978-1-003-19588-7 (ebk)

DOI: 10.4324/9781003195887

Typeset in Bembo
by Apex CoVantage, LLC

Dedication and thanks

We dedicate this book to our children, Ares sons: Kristoffer, Andreas, Nikolai and Ninas sons: Joakim, Kristoffer and Daniel

We would also like to thank all discussion partners who have contributed to this book:
Deputy Director General in the Directorate in the Norwegian Correctional Service Jan-Erik Sandlie, former Minister of Justice and now County Governor Knut Storberget, former Director at the University College of Norwegian Correctional Service (KRUS) Harald Føsker, former Department Director in the Ministry of Justice Kåre Leiksett, former Governor at Ila Prison and Detention Centre Knut Bjarkeid, former trade union leader in NFF Roar Øvrebø, former psychiatrist at Ila Prison and Detention Centre Randi Rosenqvist, head of department in Church`s City Mission Trond Henriksen, Unit Manager in Red Cross Network after serving a sentence" and Stian Estenstad in Oslo Red Cross, Head of Prison Support and Manager of Network after imprisonment.

We also give a huge thanks to:
Jordan Hyatt, Synøve Nygard Andersen, Christo Brand, Kim Ekhaugen, Maria Karine Aasen-Svensrud, Asle Aase, Farukh Qureshi, Naima Khawaja, Gaby Groff-Jensen, Doris Bakken, Harriet Wennergren Lie, Simon Greer, Joel Vaag, Ana Filipa Bettencourt Costa, Rolf Wespe, Manuel Cortes, Jan-Erik Østlie and Eva.K. Nergård for valuable input.

Thanks to the Directorate in the Norwegian Correctional Service who supported this project.

CONTENTS

Preface   xi
Foreword   xii
Prologue   xiv

1. Trond enters Halden Prison   1
2. The Scandinavian model   4
3. The missing link?   7
4. What is punishment?   11
5. Dynamic security, contact officers and the principle of normality   15
6. Quality education for prison officers   18
7. Who are the prisoners?   21
8. Recidivism rate – pick a number?   25
9. The history of the Norwegian correctional system   28
10. Halden Prison: punishment that works – change that lasts!   38
11. Trond gets a wake-up call in Halden Prison   45
12. Violent extremism, terrorism and radicalization in the prisons   49

13. The challenge of the mentally ill and the use of isolation in
    prison – criticism of Norwegian practice   57

14. Women in Norwegian prisons   65

15. Trond leaves the prison for the last time   72

16. Release to freedom – mind the gap   75

17. Little Scandinavia and other international collaboration   85

18. A peek into the future   96

    Closing remarks   103

Sources   *106*
Index   *108*

PREFACE

There is growing global interest in Scandinavian correctional services and incarceration. And since Halden Prison opened in 2010, people from all over the world have made a visit. Among them: the Norwegian king, politicians, journalists, correctional staff and even the documentary maker Michael Moore.[1]

The authors of this book met when Nina, as a journalist, visited Halden Prison and did an interview with Are, the governor there.

Our intention with this book is to show how Norway has developed one of, if not *the* most, humane correctional services in the world. And what does this mean in practice? What works well and what could be improved? We wanted to reveal the building blocks of the Norwegian correctional service and the underlying values and principles, as well as the practical implementation of these policies. We will share a historical overview of the correctional services from the time of Minister of justice Inger Louise Valle in the 1970s, passing through two later government white papers up to the present situation. We also visit the future and examine one of the most modern prison in Norway, opened in 2021. We also want to share our recent visit to "little Scandinavia" at the Pennsylvania State Correctional Institution at Chester (SCI Chester).

Together we want to provide a truly original perspective on the field – through an inspiring and accessible book, full of interviews telling the stories of the policymakers, prison officers and also some inmates' experiences. Enjoy.

Oslo – June 1, 2022 – Are Høidal and Nina Hanssen

> *It is said that no one truly knows a nation until one has been inside its jails. A nation should not be judged on how it treats its highest citizens, but its lowest ones...*
> —Nelson Mandela, former inmate and president of South Africa,
> in *Long Walk to Freedom* (2008)

FOREWORD

Normality in the abnormal

Imagine what kind of expectations you, I and society have for criminal care. Consider the word. Care. At international meetings, several justice ministers told me that it is so typical and so right in Norway to call the prisons and the penal system "criminal care." It creates expectations of something more than sheer punishment. Something more than just inflicting torment on someone, as the professor of criminology and social scientist Nils Christie defined "punishment." It creates expectations. To something more than torment. I wondered as a criminal lawyer, wondered as a Minister of Justice, and I still wonder: so sky-high expectations of punishment are that it should reduce crime, deter and get the perpetrator back on track.

And then, huge expectations of change, in a system that in structure, idea, and building (prisons) originates from the early 19th century. I often asked: how can we expect change, when the system itself has not changed significantly? When the prisoners are locked up in an old prison cell, they in fact sit in the same conditions that met prisoners back in the 19th century. Very strange. Society has undergone so much change in general: in medicine to get people healthy, in substance-abuse care to get people drug-free, within school to get people competent and ready for professional life, in business to create value or in public administration to create better lives.

This was part of the reason why in the Stoltenberg government in 2005 we pointed to criminal justice and correctional services as one of our important projects. Reforms were needed here! As a social democrat, I believe reform in criminal care is social democracy in practice. Rethink. Reform. Distribute fairly. See those "at the bottom of the table." React. Create change. Create security.

We knew it wasn't necessarily going to be a victory politically. Perhaps political leadership could show that the population saw the value of reforms? Should we dare to challenge established truths and populist solutions? Should we dare to stand up in the media? I was fully aware that the simplest solution often is not always the best. To simply suggest more of the old medicine like stricter prison sentences that seldom work would make life easy without curing the problem. In the parliaments and in politics, it is difficult to vote against proposals for harsher penalties. I never suffered defeat in politics on more money for the police and harsher sanctions. Few questioned whether it worked. Few thought it seemed to work against it purpose. For politics, the prison sentence has a good deal of latent functions, as forensic-psychology professor Thomas Mathiesen described in his book on the court and society. Functions that were not necessarily motivated by the need for individual change but that met other political needs.

Mathiesen described, among other things, latent functions such as contributing to derailment; get focus away from other political needs such as health care, remove political demands for fairer distribution or actually take away the political spotlight on other types of crime that are not detected, be it economic crime or violence against women. Then it was easier to catch the street criminal; and get effective political gain. Not soft, but hard on crime.

Another latent feature of politics is being able to show action. When the Minister of Justice proposes doubling the penalties for rape, it seems appropriate. Whether it helps is another matter.

Moreover, a third latent function in the justification for the prison sentence is to conduct pure renovation. Imprisoning drug users in open urban space brings them out of sight and out of mind. They become less problematic for politicians while in Oslo prisons than in the square outside the Parliament.

It was therefore important for us in the design of a better correctional facility to dare to challenge political dynamics. This was the reason for the work on White Paper No. 37, on a punishment that works to involve the inmates and staff in prisons, research communities, and five to six other ministries and volunteer organizations. Normality was to be brought into the prisons. Also a paradox: spend so much resources on creating abnormality, and then spend all the more on bringing normality in. For example, offers of training/school to all inmates, libraries and cultural services in all prisons, social-service markets in prisons, substance-abuse units and no release to homelessness. The families and children of the inmates were to be met with family homes and childcare.

Finally, alternative forms of reaction such as juvenile punishment, community punishment, electronic monitoring and forms of reaction with a stronger influence of restorative justice should be developed. Here we quickly saw another great potential: a possibility that the convict actually made up for himself and repaired damage where possible. It's victim-friendly to react differently. The form of reaction could actually take care of the victim's desire for recognition and regret to a much greater extent than locking up contributed to. Several prisoners have expressed that next time they choose prison instead, the alternative punishment became too harsh. In that way, new criminal care can transform established myths about the real content of what it means to be "tough on crime."

I am really pleased that alternating political regimes in Norway since my time have not chosen to reverse, although the intensity of politics in this area can be discussed. Change in policy does not go without debate, public enlightenment, reflection, and leadership politically and in the sector. This book contributes to this. We would not have been able to carry out the construction of Halden Prison or the reforms in White Paper No. 37 without leaders such as prison director Are Høidal. Managers and employees like him give you a good feeling and confidence in political leadership positions. In fact, it took an officer like Høidal to create an understanding that the keys in the cluster they carry can actually also be used to unlock. As Minister of Justice, I am incredibly grateful to have had such people to pull bills of exchange. They really make a difference, creating optimism for the future of correctional services.

By Knut Storberget
County Governor, Former Minister of Justice (2005–2011)

PROLOGUE

"This is not a prison. I can hardly see the difference between the prison officers and the inmates here.[2] What? Do the prisoners also have their own bath, TV and a fridge?"[3]

Christo Brand, the man who says this, was a prison officer in South Africa. He was an officer while Nelson Mandela was in prison on both Robben Island and later Pollsmoor prison, until he was released.

I have known Brand for several years, but until now, I have never seen him so confused.

We are visiting one of Norway's highest-security jails, Halden Prison, opened formally in 2010 by the Norwegian King Harald V. He seems almost speechless. Brand looks again at governor Are Høidal and me with big, surprised eyes. He hardly believes what he sees and hears.

"Welcome to Halden Prison and the Norwegian correctional service. This is the way we do it here," Høidal replies.

Høidal has worked in different positions in the Norwegian prison service for more than 27 years and has broad practical experience from the history of correctional services in Norway.

A few months before this visit, Brand personally guided me on a visit to Robben Island outside Cape Town. He gave me the story about how, during apartheid, he secretly formed a relationship with the world's most famous prisoner: Nelson Mandela.[4]

As a journalist I am always curious about the details surrounding how the two men, the prison officer and the prisoner, formed a close relationship and how the prison officer helped Mandela to see his grandchild in a prison where children were not allowed.

Later Mandela told him that the minutes alone with his grandson where he could smell and hug the little baby did a lot for his wellbeing and gave him hope. His hope endured and later the world's most famous prisoner became the president of South Africa.

The huge contrast between the situation on Robben Island during apartheid and Halden Prison today, which is referred to as one of the most humane high-security prisons in the world, is enormous. Brand speaks slowly.

"On my first day as a prison officer in South Africa, a prisoner killed another prisoner. Then he tore out the victim's heart and ate it in front of the others. I was shocked," he says quietly and looks down. "These kinds of situations were quite usual at the time," Brand says with a lower voice.[5]

The Norwegian governor Høidal and his staff listen carefully while we walk through the big prison kitchen with a training restaurant, where prisoners are preparing food. Brand's eyes grow large when he notices all the big sharp knives and equipment.

PHOTO 0.1 Christo Brand was Nelson Mandelas prison officer and friend. In 2020, he visited Halden prison

Source: Photo: Nina Hanssen

Høidal says that the situation in the Norwegian prison has gone through a big change and that everything was different when he started to serve in the Norwegian prison service in the early 80s.

Høidal adds "At that time we had a masculine, macho culture with focus on guarding and security. And the recidivism rate (people who come back for new crimes after completing their original sentences) showed that 63% of those given "unconditional" prison sentences reoffended within five years of being released. For people with three or more previous sentences, the re-offense rate was closer to 80%."[6]

In 1980 the Norwegian Correctional Service (NCS) was established as a national-level governmental agency responsible for the implementation of all criminal sentences and pretrial detentions in Norway. The first decade was characterized by multiple challenges.

On March 4, 1989, a female prison officer at Ila Prison in Oslo was killed by an inmate during a temporary leave from prison to visit the cinema outside. In December 1991, another prison officer was killed in Sarpsborg Prison,[7] Høidal remembers. He says restrictions were put in place to increase the safety of the workers. Later Norway underwent a rigorous series of reforms to focus less on punishment and more on the rehabilitation of prisoners.

"We started offering prisoners daily training and educational programs and we were excited that the role of the prison officers was going to be completely changed. It was a paradigm shift," Høidal says. Høidal has worked in several positions in the criminal-justice system, but when he talks about Halden Prison he talks with passion and love like a father talking about his child.

When they officially opened the prison in 2010, Høidal had to show the new modern prison to Knut Storberget, the Minister of Justice, and King Harald V of Norway. Maybe this was the first

xvi Prologue

PHOTO 0.2   When Halden Prison opened in 2010 both King Harald (in the middle) and the Minister of Justice Knut Storberget(to the left) was there. Governor Are Høidal is on the right side.

Source: Photo: Jan-Erik Østlie

and only visit a royal had made into a prison. The visitors even visited one of the inmates in a cell. According to Storberget, the King sat down on the bed and was quite surprised that the man beside him had killed someone.[8]

In Halden Prison there are around 252 male inmates today. So far nobody has escaped. In the middle of the prison area there is a small house where fathers can stay with their family from 24 to 48 hours when they have completed the program "fathers in prison." The aim of this program is to motivate male inmates with kids for their role as a parent when they are released.

Halden Prison has a library, a gym, a kitchen, and different places for inmates to work or study. Officers and prisoners are together during all activities.

"They eat together, play football together, do leisure activities together and this allows us to really interact with prisoners, to talk to them and to motivate them. The positive relations between the officers and the prisoners is important and part of our dynamic security (Read the definition on Dynamic Security here:)"[9] Høidal says.

> "The main rule in Section 17 of the Norwegian Penal Code is that all inmates in Norwegian prisons should, as far as practically possible, be allowed company of other inmates and officers during work, training, programming, and in their leisure periods. This basically means access to community and social contact with other prisoners all day, from morning to evening"[10]
>
> *(Lobel & Smith, 2019)*

In addition to the focus on dynamic security, the principle of normality, which is defined in the European Prison rules,[11] is also one of the cornerstones for the Scandinavian prison service. The prisoners have voting rights and access to public services from local and municipal service providers to the prison.

> "The principle of normality – the idea that life inside prison should be as close as possible to life in the community – is one of the cornerstones of the modern Norwegian correctional system"
> We always have in mind that mostly all inmates will be released one day, and maybe become your neighbour?
>
> *(Høidal, 2018, p. 58).*[12]

Brand walks around the prison compound which covers an area of 27,000 square meters, and with walls surrounding a total area of 37 acres including a small forest and other green spaces. He is told

PHOTO 0.3 Christo Brand, Nelson Mandela's prison officer and friend, visits Halden Prison

Source: Photo: Nina Hanssen.

PHOTO 0.4 Nelson Mandelas prison officer Christo Brand visited Halden Prison in 2021. Here with the governor Are Høidal and Nina Hanssen

Source: Photo: Frode Erlandsen.

that the distance between the walls and the surrounding forest, the unobstructed visibility zone, is the same. He is surprised by what he sees and hears when he speaks to the prisoners in their cells and in the car-repair workshop. It is an open atmosphere in this high-security prison, and the tone is relaxed. He had heard about the Scandinavian welfare model, but he did not know about the correctional service.

Brand wants to spread the word about the Norwegian correctional service, its normality principle[13] and how the dynamic security works in practice.

"I really did not know you could run a prison this way. I believe that this is unique and might inspire prison officers and leaders all over,"[14] Christo Brand says before he leaves Norway, adding: "I will be back."

Notes

1. More, Michael visit Norwegian Prison – Michael Moore – YouTube.
2. Hanssen, N. (2020). Da Nelson Mandelas fangevokter kom inn i det norske fengselet, fikk han seg en overraskelse | FriFagbevegelse.
3. Personal communication with Brand, C., Halden prison, January 13, 2020.
4. Hanssen, N. (2019). Bistandsaktuelt Sør-Afrika: Tidligere innsatte vil ikke forlate fangeøya Robben Island (bistandsaktuelt.no). Personal communication with Christo Brand at Robben Island in South Africa 2019.
5. Personal communication with Christo Brand January 2020
6. Meglestue, I. (1996). Stadig flere pådrar seg ny straffereaksjon, Samfunnspeilet 1996, page 3 (www.ssb.no).
7. Høidal, Are FSR3101_09_Hoidal 58..66 (unit.no).
8. Personal communication with Knut Storberget, 2021.
9. Dynamic Security is the concept of prison staff actively and frequently observing and interacting with prisoners to gain a better understanding and awareness of prisoners and assessing the risks that they represent (UN, 2013). Personal communication with Are Høidal 2020.

10. Prisoners' Association as an Alternative to Solitary Confinement – Lessons Learned from a Norwegian High-Security Prison by Are Høidal in (2019–12–12). Lobel, J., & Smith, P. (Eds.). (2019). *Solitary confinement: Effects, practices, and pathways toward reform.* Oxford: Oxford University Press. Retrieved January 10, 2022, from https://oxford.universitypressscholarship.com/view/10.1093/oso/9780190947927.001.0001/oso-9780190947927.
11. The Council of Europe's recommendation on Prison Rules (2006) part 1, number 2: "Life in prison shall approximate as closely as possible the positive aspects of life in the community."
12. Høidal, A. (2018). Normality behind the walls: Examples from Halden Prison. *Federal Sentencing Reporter, 31*(1), 58–66. https://doi.org/10.1525/fsr.2018.31.1.58.
13. The Normality principle was established by the 1951 committee, which stated: Detention must be carried out such that it, to the greatest possible degree, reflects condition in the free world, to prepare the inmate for life after release and to counteract the harmful effects of imprisonment.
14. United Nations DPKO: Prison Incident Management Handbook, 2013, p. 26.

1
TROND ENTERS HALDEN PRISON

He can feel the wind trying to take hold of his coat, as he helps himself out of the taxi. In Norway the convicts travel to the prison with public transport or taxi. Trond Henriksen (45) was known in the media as one of Norway's most dangerous prisoners. He had kidnapped a policeman and a security officer when he tried to escape from jail as a 26-year-old drug addict with several robberies on his record. The man with the dark fluffy hair and thick dark eyebrows, charming beauty mole on his cheek and often-sparkling blue eyes is well known from several media articles and TV documentaries.

But today his eyes are blurry and he feels weak and a bit shaky. When he gets a glimpse of the cold, gray, six-meter-high concrete wall, which stretches all the way round this brand new prison in Halden, he feels depressed. He has recently read in the newspapers that this is a modern prison, and that even King Harald himself opened it earlier this year.

Halden Prison seems to be the first prison in history that was opened in the presence of someone from the royal family.

Well then, he thinks, *I have never opened a prison, but I have visited far more prisons than the King of Norway.*

Trond walks away so that the security camera cannot catch him. He knows where those kinds of things are placed.

Just one more, he thinks, drawing out a syringe and filling it up with heroin. Getting stoned, "filling up the tank," that is exactly what he wants now that he is about to start serving his next prison sentence. He was about 14 years old when he was first imprisoned and has spent about 16 years in different Norwegian prisons. This time he deliberately applied to Halden because he knew they have a substance-abuse program. Besides, he knew the prison director from before.

He can feel the heroin starting to work and walks slowly towards the gate to be registered. He is humming a song from his favorite group the Rolling Stones while he just lets himself float. After the body search and all the other intake routines – by now he has gotten so used to it – he gets locked in his cell in department A. The world turns like a merry-go-round as he lies down on the bed.

This was my last syringe stick, he tells himself. *This is going to be my last imprisonment. I do not want this kind of life anymore. Enough is enough.*

When he stood waiting outside Halden Prison some hours earlier, he was totally exhausted. He had no place to live after he ended up with strong abstinence from not having his drugs in a cell in a Swedish prison on the border. He had not managed to deal with the divorce from his former wife, and he had even tried to commit suicide.[1]

DOI: 10.4324/9781003195887-1

Now that should be enough! he thought. Why did it end up like this?

He grew up in Oslo, the capital of Norway, with his mother and a little sister. They lived in a municipal apartment, and they did not have much money. He was a restless boy and always felt like the class clown. When he, as a 12-year-old boy, tried out hashish for the first time, he was sure he would die. This is because his mother had told him that if you use narcotics you will die.

But something else also happened that year, something that was going to have an important influence on his life. One day he did not have enough money to pay for the bus, but he was lucky that an elderly man offered him a lift. Tragically, that man sexually abused him. This affected him so deeply, but he did not manage to tell anyone about it until 38 years later. It disturbed his mindset, and for a long period of time he hated homosexuals. It was shortly after this incident that Trond, who was 14 years old, was imprisoned for the first time. He was put in a double cell and was scared to death.

After being released and then imprisoned a couple of times, he started using heroin.

The prison governor Are Høidal knows this special prisoner. He remembered that he was responsible for the first prisoner revolt in Oslo Prison, when the then law student Are Høidal worked as a temporary officer in a prison of which he later would become the head. This time he decides to send Trond to a hospital where he can stay a week for detoxing. It is not difficult for the prison director to see that Trond is now in a very bad state. He was not the same person who he knew at the end of the 90s in Oslo prison, he was not the same confident man who was even given for a period the task of motivating other prisoners. Despite his long criminal career and imprisonments, Trond experienced many good periods. He is open about his good and bad sides. He has become a media favorite and was even the main character in the documentary "Grown-Up Boys Don't Cry." This documentary is a film about the project called Stifinneren (The pathfinder), a unique Norwegian project between prison authorities and the drug institution Tyrilistiftelsen. They worked with young drug addicts, and the project was inspired by a program in New York. Trond has also, more than once, participated in KROM conferences together with prison directors and top bureaucrats in the Ministry of Justice.[2] KROM is an annual conference which is unique in the world, as prison authorities discuss prisoners' issues with the prisoners, and even go skiing for three-hour intermissions before the next discussion.

When Trond returns from the hospital he is invited to participate in the official opening of the substance-abuse unit in the prison. Trond has also, on several occasions, met the Minister of Justice, Knut Storberget (Labor Party) who will now come to open the substance-abuse unit.

You are not to be ashamed

When Trond last met Storberget, he promised he would stop his criminal career.

"Never again," he said then, and the Minister was satisfied. That Storberget now will see that he is back behind bars and in the substance-abuse unit makes him embarrassed. He feels so ashamed. He has fallen again. The Minister of Justice comes into his room; he is alone and sits down on the bed. Trond is surprised. Then the Minister says:

> "You know Trond, you shall not be ashamed. The most human thing to do is to fail. You must never forget that!"

These words ease the enormous pressure inside Trond. As a prisoner who is choking back the tears, it means so much to get a friendly pat on his shoulder from the Minister of Justice – the head of all prisons – before he walks out again.

Three months later, Trond has completed the substance-abuse program. The prison director asks if he wants to launch the radio program "Radio Inside" via the FM connection, a program that can be listened to even by people in the local community. Trond says yes without hesitation. Here he can utilize all his capabilities. Here he thinks he can enjoy himself – yes, and perhaps he can even get access to work in the media.

Trond is grateful to the employees who saw the potential in him and never gave up. He believes that if we give people responsibility, we give them trust. Responsibility gives him great confidence. This opportunity gives people the chance to really make a change.

Know me from within! The outside says nothing about me.
Sohil, Prisoner in Ullersmo Prison, 2021

Notes

1. Trond Henriksen, Personal Communications, 2021.
2. KROM.no.

2
THE SCANDINAVIAN MODEL

The Norwegian correctional service is different from those of most other countries, which is one of the reasons why it attracts a lot of attention from abroad. Does Norway have one of the world's most humane correctional services? And what does this mean in practice?

Norway with a population of only 5.4 million people,[1] one of highest GDPs in the world and recognized as having a high quality of life, can be a model for a global penal reform.

In addition to great achievements in winter sports, Norway is known as a cradle-to-grave welfare state funded in part by large reserves of oil and natural gas.

Since discovering oil, Norway, a social democracy, has invested wisely in creating a welfare state, which includes the world's largest pension fund. This gives Norwegians security in crises and everyday life.

Myths about Norway

There are many myths about Norway and the Vikings in the north. Maybe you have heard that Norway is #1 in the world for electric-vehicle adoption? Or maybe the first thing you think of is a country with mountains, fjords, trolls and salmon? But most importantly for this book, in this tiny country – which is part of Scandinavia – we also believe that penal policies are intrinsically linked to social policies. Before we take a deep dive into trying to understand the country's correctional system, we must look at social policies. That is important context and knowledge to help you see why the crime rates are low and why the Nordic model was referred to as the next supermodel in a 2013 article from *The Economist*.[2]

In that article, the writer says: "If you had to be reborn anywhere in the world as a person with average talents and income, you would want to be a Viking. The Nordics cluster at the top of world charts of everything from economic competitiveness to social health and happiness. They have avoided both southern Europe's economic sclerosis and America's extreme inequality." But the article fails to explain the important role of the three equal partners in the uniquely Norwegian tripartite model in working life: between authorities, employer organizations and trade unions. Tripartite cooperation has a long history in Norway. It started in 1932 when the Confederation of Trade Union (LO Norway) and the national Labor Party presented a crisis program demanding that everybody in Norway should have a job.

DOI: 10.4324/9781003195887-2

PHOTO 2.1 Einar Gerhardsen was a Norwegian politician from the Labour Party of Norway. He was the 22nd prime minister of Norway for three periods

Source: Photo: ARBARK

First main agreement was the foundation

In 1935, the first main agreement between LO and the employers laid the foundation for the Norwegian tripartite cooperation model. Even if they disagree, they have respect and trust between them. The results in the years that followed were economic growth and social reforms.

From cradle to grave

The vision of a welfare state that provided the people with social security from "cradle to grave" was initiated in 1945 when the German occupants left Norway after the second world war. The

Norwegian Labor Party also won the election after the war and held power in government for a long period until 1965.

This gave the labor movement the opportunity to realize its political project, a society that we can see today with a comprehensive welfare system and a working life characterized by strong organizations and close party cooperation.

This model has helped to bring about changes in working life, strengthened competitiveness, and provided productivity growth, increased prosperity and skills development.

Norway has become one of the richest countries in Europe (average annual earnings 609,600 NOK),[3] with the lowest unemployment (3.1% in February 2022)[4] and a constructive social dialogue between employees and employers.

This is achieved through tools such as:

1. Strong partners in the workplace
2. High degree of gender equality (almost as many women in work as men)
3. Main agreement of 1935.

And the results are:

1. Small income differences
2. High degree of union organization
3. Low unemployment.

In 2022, Norway was ranked as having the world's highest productivity rate GDP (PPP) per hour: $75.08.[5]

American senator Bernie Sanders boosted and promoted the Nordic model in an interview with ABC News in 2015.[6] At the same time, he also was verbally attacked for being a socialist, and many Americans have the idea that this is bad. But Sanders was excited that Scandinavian countries are very democratic, with free healthcare to all, free educational systems, retirement benefits and childcare more robust than the US. Sanders also mentioned the fact that the governments, by large, work for ordinary people, and the middle class has more income and wealth equality, better salaries, and a more sustainable welfare system.

Notes

1. SSB statistics 18 November 2021: Link: Befolkning (ssb.no).
2. The next supermodel | The Economist *2013*.
3. Statistics Norway (ssb.no).
4. 08930: Sysselsetting og arbeidsledighet (med endringstall). Brudd- og sesongjustert, 3-måneders glidende gjennomsnitt 2006M02 – 2022M02. Statistikkbanken (ssb.no).
5. Most Productive Countries 2022 (worldpopulationreview.com).
6. (194) Sen. Bernie Sanders Says U.S. Should Look More Like Scandinavia – YouTube.

3
THE MISSING LINK?

Is there a link between the Nordic welfare model – a social democracy in which all have jobs, equal pay and are protected through unions with a strong social-welfare "safety net" – crime and a human prison system? This has often been questioned by visitors.

Conditions in Nordic prisons have also been characterized as more humane than the conditions in prisons in other countries. Professor of Criminology at Victoria University of Wellington John Pratt has since 2008 used the term "Nordic exceptionalism," in which he includes low rates of imprisonment and humane prison conditions.[1] The term "Nordic exceptionalism" has also been central to many researchers of prisons in recent years.

The Norwegian Correctional Service focuses on the rehabilitation (versus solely punishment) of prisoners. The punishment of the individual is conducted in accordance with a plan in which both prisoner and his/her own contact officer have been involved. In the Norwegian educational system, a pupil has a dedicated contact teacher. Inmates also have a contact officer. A change of behavior and a return to society as a law-abiding citizen is the ultimate goal. And as you'll read later, the actual return to society is an important factor and also a success criterion.

The prisons systems staircase

As the Norwegian Labor Party parliamentarian in the Committee on Justice, Maria Aasen-Svendsrud[2] says: Ideally in Norway, the prisoner should be guided through a procedure that follows what we call 'the prison system's staircase.' This means that an inmate who starts in a high-security facility will progress to low security, and then to transitional housing and electronic monitoring. It is the probationary service that is responsible for the transitional housing and electronic monitoring.

The principle of normality in the correctional service means that the punishment is the restriction of liberty; no other rights have been removed by the sentencing court. Consequently, the sentenced offender has the same rights as anyone else living in Norway. Throughout the sentence, the prisoner has access to public services (schools, health, libraries, etc.). The prison imports these service providers. This is very different from other countries.

The current government (2022) in Norway says that ideally, no one should be obliged to serve their sentence under stricter circumstances than necessary for the security of the community. For this reason, offenders must be placed in the lowest possible security regime.

8 The missing link?

PHOTO 3.1 Norwegian Labor politician Maria Karine Aasen-Svensrud visits Ila prison
Source: Photo: Nina Hanssen

During the serving of a sentence, life inside should resemble life outside as far as possible. When a prisoner comes out of prison, it is the responsibility of the local authorities to plan and organize this person's return to the community.

It should also be mentioned that Norway has a very active and strong voluntary sector, which contributes to many aspects of reintegration efforts. That said, it is the probation service and, finally, the local authority which are ultimately responsible.

The "principle of proximity" is also very important for the return to society. This principle states that the inmate should serve their sentence as close to their own home as possible and should have contact with their family and friends as much as is reasonable.

Norway strives to assess each recidivist individually. For example: a drug addict who is in prison, being rehabilitated and then released, may have a relapse, and start taking drugs again, commit another offense and end up back in prison.

However, this person does not have to start all over again from scratch. Experience from the previous rehabilitation is considered in determining the content of the further detention process.

One final specific point is that in Norway, a previously convicted person does not have to mention this previous conviction in a job application (except in professions where previously good conduct is asked for and required). This undoubtedly makes it easier to get back to a normal life, where individuals can support themselves financially.

In Aasen-Svensrud's view, this is about the broader community's ability not only to respond to crime, but also to recognize its share of the responsibility for the crime. This may include lack of social mobility, failure in school, unemployment, or children and adolescents not receiving adequate protection from violent environments, such as violence in close relationships and violence in the local community.

In short, the Labor Party believes that the execution of remands and prison sentences in Norway reflects both the individual's responsibility for his or her actions, and the society's responsibility for the individual's ability to live a law-abiding life.

The last section might appear somewhat philosophical and lofty, but I believe it reflects a basic attitude in Norwegian society which may differ from many other countries.

As already stated, there is an increased interest in the Scandinavian welfare model, but the interest also includes the Scandinavian correctional system. In *Scandinavian Penal History, Culture and Prison Practice*, a book edited by Peter Scarff Smith and the Norwegian criminologist Thomas Ugelvik, several contributors undertake historical and cross-disciplinary studies to critically examine penal practices in Scandinavia. The book paints a much more nuanced picture of the welfare policies, ideologies and social control in states. Smith and Ugelvik (2019)[3] say that visiting Scandinavian prisons together with foreign visitors has shown them that not everything is simply black and white, and that differences are sometimes perhaps more a matter of cultural context and background. The authors have even observed foreign researchers reacting with a certain disappointment after visiting progressive, seemingly exceptional and initially very humane-looking Scandinavian institutions, when discovering that, after all, these places are still prisons, places of detention where people are deprived of their liberty and subjected to strict rules and regulations.[4] They further mentioned that there has also been a change in the Scandinavian welfare state, and that the crisis and neo-human ideology has transferred the original egalitarian social democratic model to a greater or lesser extent (Smith & Ugelvik, 2019). Some talk about not only the rise but also the fall of the welfare state with Nordic countries suffering from increased poverty as well as greater social and economic inequality.

The importance of the trade-union movement

As early as 1923, the employees of the Norwegian correctional services established a nationwide trade union called the Norwegian Prison and Probation Association (NFF). The Norwegian Correctional Service may never have been what it is without this association having followed this development closely. As the association's 100th anniversary book states: "And this development, which deserves the designation of a silent revolution, would not have been possible without a trade union that organizes large sections of the agency's employees. Over the 100 years it has existed, the union has fought not only for wages and working conditions for its members, but to the best of its ability also for the prison conditions. No prisoners, no prison either. Nor any probation office."[5]

There has been a shift in political direction in Norway with the conservative government between 2016–2020, with flat cuts and more privatization and less resources for the public sector, but still the Nordic welfare model is strong and so is the prison service.

Notes

1. Pratt, J. (2008). Scandinavian exceptionalism in an era of penal excess: Part I: The nature and roots of Scandinavian exceptionalism. *The British Journal of Criminology, 48*(2), 119–137. https://doi.org/10.1093/bjc/azm072; Pratt, J. (2007). Scandinavian exceptionalism in an era of penal excess: Part II: Does Scandinavian exceptionalism have a future? *The British Journal of Criminology, 48*(3), 275–292. https://doi.org/10.1093/bjc/azm073
2. Personal communication Maria Aasen-Svensrud February 2022.
3. *Scandinavian Penal History, Culture and Prison Practice*, a book edited by Peter Scarff Smith and the Norwegian criminologist Thomas Ugelvik, 2019 Palgrave MacMillan.
4. Scharff Smith, P., &Ugelvik, T. (2017). *Scandinavian Penal History, Culture and Prison Practice*, page 6, Springer.
5. Østlie, Jan-Erik, *A Silent Revolution*, page 401.

4
WHAT IS PUNISHMENT?

The forms and content of punishment vary from country to country, depending on economic, religious, cultural, social, and political conditions. Norway has, over the years, built up a modern welfare state and a well-functioning correctional service, although much remains to be done.

In Norway, an average of 289,000 convictions are imposed each year. Only around 9,000 of these apply to prison sentences; other sanctions are various forms of community punishment, including special sanctions for youth, home detention and fines and confiscations.

As of February 1, 2022, there were 3,097 inmates in Norwegian prisons.

In Norway, punishment has been defined by law professor Johs. Andenæs as follows: "Punishment is a harm that the state inflicts on an offender for the purpose of making it feel like an harm." The Supreme Court has since endorsed this view.

The task and structure of the Correctional Service are authorized by law and include both the prison service and the probation service. The Ministry of Justice and Public Security is politically responsible, and operational management is exercised by the Norwegian Directorate of Correctional Services in cooperation with regions and local management.

The social mission of the Correctional Service is to carry out sanctions handed down by the courts and to keep accused persons in custody, as determined by prosecutors or courts. Sanctions have several purposes. The purpose of the punishment is twofold. On the one hand, we have the general contraception that will give citizens a clear understanding of what is legal and illegal behavior, and that should make sure that society is protected from crime and ensure the safety of the population. On the other hand, we have the individual preventive, which has three main aspects. The convicted shall be prevented from committing new offences by imposed detention. Convicts shall perceive the punishment and detention as negative and thus refrain from committing new criminal acts. After that, arrangements shall be made for the convict to make his/her own efforts during imprisonment to counteract new offences.

Inmates should know that they risk punishment for offences, and that the punishment should be perceived as harm but have a rehabilitative effect.

In the 1960s and onwards, there was a strong belief that rehabilitation and treatment had a positive effect. Many still believe in this. Nevertheless, some of the research of the time showed that treatment efforts mostly did not work on inmates in American prisons. It gave rise to the concept "Nothing works," which was eventually considered a truth, regardless of time and place. A counterreaction came later.

Researchers and clinicians from Canada documented that therapy and learning could have a certain effect, presuming that adapted methods and techniques were used. "Nothing works" was

DOI: 10.4324/9781003195887-4

replaced by "What works." Canadian correctional services developed many programs, some of which were imported to Norway. In Norway, the idea of rehabilitation has always been strong, although criminal-policy fluctuations have resulted in varying degrees of financial appropriations for this.

In Norwegian correctional services, the "what works" idea was given a central place. Several White Papers on correctional services confirm this. It is part of a unified picture that democratic and humanistic anchoring helped Justice Minister Knut Storberget (Minister of State from 2005–2011) to use "Punishment that works" (2007–2008)[1] as the motto for the future of correctional services. The punishing element should be various movement and freedom restrictions that follow from sentencing, from high security on the one hand, to electronic monitoring and community punishment on the other. The new penal code states, among other things: "The consideration of justice and humanity speaks against inflicting harm on people without it having any usefulness for society."

"Punishment as an harm" is enshrined in White Paper 37 (Storberget report). Section 3, Choice of Values, section 3.1. states the purpose of the penalty:

> "The intended effects of the punishment can be divided into three main groups. Measures that are intended to be individual preventive as to prevent new offences by using deprivation of liberty (incapacitation), deterrent measures and improvement measures. Through deterrent measures, the punishment shall also have a general preventive effect, and in the long run this shall create a positive attitude in society. Maintaining the social calm is also a purpose of punishment."[2]

Some measures are broader and include all convicts, regardless of where the sentence is carried out.

Consequently, punishment is probably meant to be perceived as harm – not least because one hopes that it will be a deterrent to future offences.

The low recidivism in Norway shows that this works. On a world scale, Norway has a relatively low recidivism rate, but as we will see in the chapter on recurrence and relapse, there is also disagreement about how this is measured.

PHOTO 4.1 The former department director of the Ministry of Justice Kaare E. Leiksett is still very engaged in prison policy. Here in a discussion with Jan-Erik Sandlie, the deputy Director General in the Directorate of Norwegian Correctional Service in the summer of 2022

Source: Photo: Nina Hanssen

The cross-political trend in Norway today (2022) is probably clear. Punishment shall feel like harm. I don't think there's any country that's yet found a good alternative to prison, so I'm sure we'll have these institutions for many years to come. Nevertheless, in Norway we can see an increase in the use of community sentences, often as an alternative to serving time in open prisons. In all cultures and traditions, there are written and unwritten norms for what a society can let pass without anyone reacting. We can assume that material and social conditions explain quite a bit about what can be accepted in a society. In Norway, we have the penal code to deal with and we have experienced that what is preventive regarding crime is healthy relationships, good networks, education, and opportunities for help.

Everyday life varies quite a bit in Norwegian correctional services today, and several prisons stand out positively. It is generally accepted that imprisonment and other sanctions shall be based on the handed-down sentence. Double punishment is illegal in Norway, such as confiscation of leave rights without factual justification.

Among the prisons with high security that stand out is Halden Prison, which deliberately and purposefully has worked with normalization as a principle, something you can read more about in the chapter on Halden Prison. "Normalization" means that life in prison should, as far as possible, resemble life outside.

The entire correctional service wants to work according to the following principles.[3]

1. The most important principle is that the interaction between employees and inmates must follow common forms of interaction between people. Respect for each other's distinctive character and characteristics shall be met with openness, discussion and understanding.
Interactions and activities are founded on humanity and values enshrined in human rights, and can only be deviated from if a difficult situation cannot be resolved without the use of physical force. Dynamic security is what is created in interaction between people and appears through everyday events and routines. The role of civil servants which was presented in the 1990s is reminiscent of the one found among environmental therapists in other institutions. It is intentional.
2. Convicts are not deprived of their rights to education, health services, social services, housing, work, etc. In Norwegian correctional services, public services are available to all convicts, both those serving time in prison and those serving community sentences. Experienced employees in the agency provide the necessary assistance to ensure that the rights are met. The scheme shows that the convicts' need for assistance is a social task, not just a job for the Correctional Service.
3. Schooling, training and other educational activities shall be up-to-date and appropriate. There is hardly any benefit to be gained from offering training that is not applicable and relevant outside of prison. Public, voluntary and private educational providers will be considered, as the interests and preferences of prisoners are as diverse as those of most people.
4. A final understanding of the principle of normalization is expressed through what one might slightly imprecisely call normal expectations of convicts. The starting point is that you apply common expectations, use familiar words and concepts and generally interact in the ordinary way. If that is insufficient, appropriate measures shall be taken to compensate for any difficulties.

Convicts are not a uniform group. However, repeated surveys show that they have more social and personal problems and that their problems are more pervasive than for the average population. This applies first and foremost to the repeat offenders, and the biggest problems are for those who can be considered the sickest inmates.

Need for new measures

Some inmates have very poor functioning and partly massive mental-health challenges. Some are psychotic, others may be brain-damaged, mentally disabled or for other reasons unable to meet "normal expectations" in prison care.

Former prison director Knut Bjarkeid at Ila Prison and psychiatrist Randi Rosenqvist have for years claimed that other and more appropriate measures are needed, and that this group is most harmed by imprisonment.

Notes

1. Report no. 37 (2007-2008) – regjeringen.no.
2. Report no. 37 (2007-2008) (regjeringen.no).
3. Personal communication with Kåre Leiksett 2022.

5
DYNAMIC SECURITY, CONTACT OFFICERS AND THE PRINCIPLE OF NORMALITY

One of the most noticeable and special characteristics of the Norwegian correctional system is the relationship between prisoners and prison officers. But how is this possible without affecting security?

There are different security systems in Norwegian prisons, but it is a clear goal that no one should be subject to a more severe punishment than necessary.

Security in the penal system is the sum of the means which are employed to prevent and control situations in which the security of society, employees and the convicted can be at risk.

Such tools are, amongst other things, accurate assessment of risk, leadership training, physical training, training in handling unwanted events, correct handling of information about prisoners, systematic control activity and good contingency plans to ensure the security of everyone.

In most high-security prisons, there are both exterior fences and walls, locked doors, and surveillance cameras. This is called static security. In Norway, prison officers are not armed. They can use handcuffs, batons and in special cases CS gas. In low-security prisons, only low fences are used.

The most unusual is the use of dynamic security[1] in practical everyday prison life. Dynamic security involves the relationship between people and is used deliberately in security work. Today, prison officers must be out in the unit among the prisoners to take care of security while they at the same time give instructions to the prisoners. The prison officers participate in making food, they work together with the prisoners and they help them with practical things. Norwegian dynamic security is characterized by the fact that prison officers, by participating in activities together with the prisoners and the convicted, collect information and establish relationships which are useful in efforts to inspire and motivate, as well as in conducting risk assessment.

This presumes that prison officers are present and form relationships. While the prison officers can establish relationships, it is important to be aware that they deal with people in difficult situations and that they have and use authority. Occasionally it can be difficult to work in a system with the use of force while one tries to motivate prisoners. The balance between being personal and professional is difficult and demands skill in managing relationships.

The development of the prison officers' role

In the White Paper number 27 (1997–1998) the values and principles for the future penal system were presented. One of the core values was "Fulfilment should be based on individual needs and premises and support the convicted in his desire to stop criminal activity." The principle that follows is that "the penal system should contribute to strengthening self-respect and the ability to handle everyday life and to stimulate the will to take responsibility for life itself."

The individual prisoner is responsible for his own behavior and choices but the penal system shall arrange things so that the individual can find the correct path. The prison officers should have a central role: "They are to be inspirers, influencers, and facilitators. They should give directions and motivate the convicted and make an environment that stimulates the development of new skills." This represents a remarkable change in terms of the traditional prison officer's role.

On this basis, there should be an increased focus on individually adapted correction. The prisoners' needs should determine the type of prison that is chosen for them. The placement and regime within the prison should be determined by a similar judgement. As much as possible, the prisoners should be differentiated in terms of type of criminal behavior, potential danger for the community and individual needs. Simultaneously, the differentiation should result in a pathway from closed to open imprisonment within and across ranges of sentencing alternatives.

No one should serve under stricter conditions than necessary for security. Prisoners with sentences longer than six months should serve under conditions according to a plan presented when the sentence begins. This plan should be based on an analysis of the reasons why the prisoner has engaged in criminal activity. It should form the basis for active efforts to give the prisoner knowledge, skills, and positive attitudes towards his release. The prison officer should have a central role in these efforts. Again, this represents a significant change from the prison officer's role in the 70s and 80s.

As a consequence of this more individualized imprisonment, and of the prisoner's particular needs and assumptions needing to form the basis of what type of prison and what content of sentence should be used, the professionalism of the prison officers had to be strengthened and different methods had to be developed. One of the central principles in Report 27 to parliament was "Daily life in prisons should be characterised by active cooperation between prisoners and employees." The employees should participate in the development of new forms of imprisonment and professional measures. The traditional role of prison officers should be changed. The employees should have active roles in measures which contribute to the ability of the prisoner to have a crime-free existence after his sentence is served. At the end of the 90s, cognitive theory became an essential method in the Norwegian Correctional Service. The main idea in this theory was that the thought process itself is the basis for reflection and change. By consciously considering thoughts before, during and after a crime, the offender shall consider which alternatives he had in the situation. When he or she finds himself or herself in such a situation again, the person will hopefully act differently, meaning without an offence. Many programs in prison care are now based on cognitive theory, and the prison officers are expected to run this programming enterprise. This represented a big boost for this role.

Two important tools in the work for change with inmates are the future plan and the system-of-contact prison officers, or contact officers. The plan for the future involves both the imprisonment and what should happen after release. The individual prisoner should be responsible for his own future plan, but the prison officer must be a supporter while preparing it. Here the role of the contact officer is important. There is a separate circular which describes the role of the contact officers in detail. They are expected to serve as the link between the prisoner and his environment. The contact officer shall advise the prisoner on serving his sentence, applications for leave, what kind of activities are advisable and general motivation. What was unusual when this was established was that the prisoner was also trained on what a contact officer was. There was a separate training program for this.

Dynamic security

Dynamic security presumes extensive human contact between the prison officers and the prisoner. Such close contact helps to avoid problems with discipline and makes it easier to solve such problems when they occur, unlike in other countries that might believe this can create a dangerous situation for the staff and the inmate, and that also might be afraid of this creating an environment where criminals make networks. In Norway, the authorities believe that contact promotes the possibilities for prisoners to conduct influence and motivational work, which in the long run can help to avoid recidivism. Read more about the recidivism rate in Norway in Chapter 8.

The balance between being a positive influencer and the one in charge of security can be frustrating. It makes the role of the prison officer demanding but also challenging and motivating. There is tremendous variation in the everyday life of a prison officer. As described in the chapter about the Norwegian welfare system, our penal system is based on the humane treatment of all prisoners and the belief that everyone should get a chance to change their lives. However, dynamic security is more challenging in regards to dealing with convictions with restrictions.

The principle of normality

One of the cornerstones of the modern Norwegian correctional service is the idea that life inside prison should be as close as possible to life in the community. The "Normality Principle" was established by the 1951 committee, which stated: "Detention must be carried out such that it, to the greatest possible degree, reflects conditions in the free world, to prepare the inmate for life after release and to counteract the harmful effects of imprisonment."

As a result of this reform, standards were raised, and it became possible to provide education, employment, and free-time activities in prisons. Access to leave and temporary release were also introduced. However, Norway's current and successful implementation of a correctional environment focused on normality and humane effectiveness in corrections is a relatively recent development.

Note

1. *Dynamic Security:* «The concept of prison staff actively and frequently observing and interacting with prisoners to gain a better understanding and awareness of prisoners and assessing the risks that they represent.» From the UN's Prison Incident Management Handbook, 2013.

6
QUALITY EDUCATION FOR PRISON OFFICERS

In Norway, the prison-officer role is a profession. According to Harald Føsker, the former director of the University College of Norwegian Correctional Service (KRUS) for more than 30 years, a profession is mainly characterized by the following:

1. A higher education and training, authorizing specific job performance in the relevant sector
2. Relevant competencies, knowledge, skills and attitudes
3. Ethical professional guidelines
4. Autonomy to do assessments and make decisions based on one's own discretion
5. Transform theory into practical work.[1]

PHOTO 6.1   Harald Føsker speaks to new prison officers when he was director of the University College of Norwegian Correctional Service (KRUS). The institution offers the only primary education for prison officers in Norway through an accredited two-year programme leading to the degree University College Graduate in Correctional Studies. They also offer a supplementary course for students wanting to achieve a Bachelor's Degree in Correctional Studies

Source: Photo: Jan-Erik Østlie

DOI: 10.4324/9781003195887-6

Two years of higher education

Prison officers in Norway go through two years of higher education at the University College of Norwegian Correctional Service (KRUS), where they receive full pay and are taught various subjects such as psychology, criminology, law, human rights, and ethics. "The main focus is of course the execution of sentences according to the penal code. Our education is unique in the world and we educate good professional prison officers," Harald Føsker says when we meet up. He himself deserves much of the credit for the fact that the education is at college level and that the academy has its own library, good teaching facilities and a training prison. He states that great demands are made on those who want to be prison officers in Norway. In order to qualify for the University College of Norwegian Correctional Service (KRUS), you must have the relevant education, be 20 years or older, have no penal record, have a driver's license and be in good mental and physical health.

Loyal

In addition, the applicant must pass a physical-function test which involves strength and endurance. Another quality, which is important according to Føsker, is that those who work in the penal system must loyally follow the policy determined by the parliament.
"A prison officer must be personally suitable and mature enough to handle the responsibility that is entailed in having authority and power over people in a difficult situation. At the same time, one must have a basic good attitude and values, and the belief that people can change their pattern of action," Føsker says.

Føsker admits he had enormous expectations for his students and is happy that KRUS has contributed to the professionalization of Norwegian prison officers. That hasn't always been the case.

When the educational institution was established in 1937, it was only those who already worked in prisons who received the nine-week course that was offered. When WWII began in 1940, the training center had only held three courses.

When the war ended and the country had to come to terms with the traitors who worked for the Nazis, there was extra pressure on the penal system. A prison-reform committee was established in 1951, which led to the education of prison officers being one year long. At first the school was held in Oslo Prison, but then the recruitment of student prison officers began and the education was more professionalized with both theory and practice.

In 1975, the school began to offer two-year courses in Norway. The next year a group was established to study the full educational needs of employees in the Norwegian prison system.

The need for prison officers increased in line with the increase in the prison population, and in Oslo there was a constant need for more people. In 1987 an expert group was set up to study the possibility for a three-year university education.

Harald Føsker was director of KRUS for over 30 years until 2010. He still serves as an advisor and even gives lectures in other countries around the world about how Norway was able to build up its unique education system for prison officers and a library with both Norwegian and international books and magazines which is easily accessible for students. An expanded set of competences was emphasized:

> **The capacity for change** – to have teachable and willing workers who find new knowledge and use this actively at work.
> **Knowledge on security** – which is important for all professions working with vulnerable groups in society.

Relational competence – relations in a prison cannot be understood without discussing the fact that prison is the nation's power over prisoners and that prison officers are in charge of such authority.

International knowledge – the expert group emphasized that Norwegian prison officers should see their own practice in light of how penal systems work in other places in the world so that one can learn from each other.

In 2016 the name of the institution formally became the University College of Norwegian Correctional Service (KRUS). In addition to a university education, the center now offers training in:

1. Isolation
2. Mental disorders
3. Advising
4. Radicalization
5. Change and prevention.

Note

1. Personal communication with Harald Føsker 2022.

7
WHO ARE THE PRISONERS?

There is an excess of 3,600 prisoners in Norway, distributed across 33 prison unities, with a total of 58 operative prisons. The ratio of the staff is about one to one, and in 2020 there were 102 staff to 100 inmates.

At the beginning of May 2022, the occupancy in prisons was 86.5% with a total of 3,124 inmates. 615 (20%) of the 3,124 imprisoned were in custody, 782 (25%) were foreign citizens.

1. Female inmates: 169 (5.4%)
2. Remand prisoners in prison: 149 men, eight women
3. Three inmates, one with a sentence and two in custody.

A typical prisoner in 1972

In the White Paper 104 from 1977–1978 about criminal policy, Inger Lovise Valle, the Minister of Justice, said that it is "reasonable to assume that the population in prisons in essence, consists of young men from groups whith low social status in society. Most of them have committed crimes of profit, mostly thefts."[1]

Valle's statement had been based on those who were imprisoned December 1, 1972. That day, 1,876 people were in Norwegian prisons, i.e., 42 women and 1,834 men. Of these, 1,155 were in prison, 529 were in custody and 29 carried out a prison sentence because they could not afford to pay the fines imposed on them.

In the message it further says that "the prisoners stand out in therms of social status and have in this context a great lack of ressources. As many as 496 were without permanent employment, some of them were school students, but most of them were recruits from what has to be called the bottom layer of society."[2]

The 1972 survey showed that many inmates had a low level of education as well.

A typical prisoner in 2022

From our calculations based on numbers and tables from SSB (electronic monitoring is not included) it seems the most common prisoner in Norwegian prisons today is a man 30–39 years old with Norwegian citizenship.[3]

DOI: 10.4324/9781003195887-7

22 Who are the prisoners?

Further we can assume that this average person is serving a sentence for drug crimes, abuse or violence. If we also include surveys of prisoners' living conditions we can assume that this imagined inmate has had a difficult childhood where a bad financial situation, parents with alcohol and drug addiction, and violence and abuse has been a part of everyday life. A typical inmate in 2022 probably has little or no formal education and has very little experience with working life.[4]

If we take a further look at the SSB's tables and distinguishes *types of imprisonment* – whether the inmates are serving their sentence either in prison or with GPS ankle monitors, are in custody or are serving a custodial sentence – we get different answers.

Imprisonment with electronic monitoring (e-carceration)

With the aim of reducing the prison queue and improving the convicted person's chances of leading a crime-free life, NCS introduced ankle monitoring as a pilot project in six counties in Norway in 2008. Later this became a permanent practice.

The use of electronic monitoring is regulated by the execution of the Sentences Act.[5] This execution of ankle-bracelet monitoring pursuant to section 16, paragraph two, is a form of penal execution outside prison, with the goals of promoting the ability of convicts to fulfil their social and financial obligations while serving their sentence, and helping to reduce the risk of new crime. It is the probationary service (Friomsorgen) that is responsible for electronic monitoring in Norway.

According to tables from Statistics Norway (SSB), there are more prisoners in Norway serving an alternative sentence with electronic monitoring (56%) than there are prisoners serving sentences in prison. There are more female convicts than men who choose to serve with ankle bracelets. In Norway, the probation office is responsible for this alternative punishment to prison. The probation

PHOTO 7.1 The use of imprisonment with electronic monitoring is increasing in Norway

Source: Photo: Kriminalomsorgen

service is an included part of the correctional services. The new digital control measures provide increased security for society because one knows where the convicts are at all times, and there are few relapses among those serving sentences with ankle bracelets.

There are several requirements which must be met before a person is allowed an imprisonment with electronic monitoring, also called ankle-bracelet monitoring. One of the requirements is that the convict must have housing and a school or a job to go to at daytime. Besides, the convicted himself must apply to serve his sentence with an ankle bracelet.

During the COVID-19 pandemic there was an increase in the number of convicts who served with electronic monitoring.

Half of those who are serving with ankle monitors are convicted for traffic offences, and about 18% are convicted for fraud, economic and financial crimes. Amongst those with convictions for violence and abuse, half of them are sentenced for violence and threats against officials.[6]

The increasing use of electronic control in Norway has resulted in a lot of debates and discussions about whether or not this form of punishment actually works. If we look at the NCS main figures from April 2022 NCS, we find that electronic ankle monitors are the most implemented form of punishment in society.

Does EM work?

One of the purposes of introducing electronic monitoring (EM) was to reduce the risk of new crime, and there has been some research done on recidivism and new crime in this field too. Overall, research indicates that imprisonment with ankle bracelets reduces the risk of recidivism among convicts in Norway.

A key challenge when trying to establish whether one sentence type works better (or worse) than another one is that people who serve a given sentence typically differ systematically from those who do not – also in terms of their risk of reoffending. Therefore, we often end up with "apples and pears" comparisons that are hard to make sense of. For electronic monitoring, for instance, it is important to keep in mind that the eligibility criteria are implemented to ensure that the vast majority of those who serve a sentence at home with an ankle band already have a low risk of relapse. This makes it difficult to directly compare the reoffending behavior of people who serve their sentence on EM with people who serve their sentence in prison.

In 2016, researcher Synøve Nygaard Andersen, who then worked in Statistics Norway, did research about this together with co-author Kjetil Telle. The main purpose of their analysis was to see whether the proportion of persons committing new offences after their sentences was higher or lower among those serving their sentence on electronic monitoring. They created two groups of people that were actually comparable, and they exploited the fact that the electronic-monitoring pilot program had been gradually implemented across Norway. This means that they could compare the reoffending behavior of eligible people who lived in places where electronic monitoring was available to otherwise similar people who happened to live in places where electronic monitoring was not yet available. Doing this, they found that the recidivism rate and frequency reduced somewhat if people were able to serve their prison sentences at home instead of in prison (Andersen & Telle, 2022).[7]

Despite their efforts to create more comparable comparison groups, it is difficult to be absolutely certain that their results reflect the causal impact of electronic monitoring and reoffending, and are not just a correlation. Andersen adds that saying something completely certain about what affects peoples' behavior is always difficult, but she highlights that all analyses on electronic monitoring in Norway point in the same (positive) direction.[8]

"We and others find no evidence that it is going the other way. There are always caveats to keep in mind, but overall it looks like this works," she says.[9]

Notes

1. White paper 104 from 1977–1978 about criminal policy from the government.
2. White paper 104 from 1977–1978 about criminal policy page 72.
3. SSB.
4. Utviklingen av fangebefolkningen i Norge har SSB i Norge henne. Og i tabellene i Statistikkbanken.
5. https://lovdata.no/dokument/NLE/lov/2001-05-18-21.
6. SSB fengslinger og Kriminalomsorgen.no.
7. Andersen, S. N., & Telle, K. (2022). Better out than in? The effect on recidivism of replacing incarceration with electronic monitoring in Norway. *European Journal of Criminology, 19*(1), 55–76. https://doi.org/10.1177/1477370819887515
8. www.vista-analyse.no/no/publikasjoner/evaluering-av-soning-med-fotlenke/.
9. Personal communication with Synøve Anderseen at the University of Oslo.

8
RECIDIVISM RATE – PICK A NUMBER?

Nordic countries are often seen as "exceptional" in that they have moderate punitive policies while also having low rates of crime and recidivism. Compared to most other countries, Norwegian correctional services are human. Conditions in Nordic prisons are often characterized as more humane than those in other countries: an aspect of what is often referred to as "Nordic penal exceptionalism" (Pratt, 2008).[1]

"Recidivism is usually defined along the lines of a 'falling back' or 'relapse' into previous criminal behavior by a person known to have committed at least one previous offense" (cf. Blumstein & Larson, 1971, p. 124; Maltz, 2001, p. 84).[2]

Whether or not previous offenders commit new criminal acts can, among other things, tell us something about the effectiveness of the criminal-justice system. Knowledge of recidivism can be used to assess which programs and schemes work the way society wants: information that can help to further develop the current criminal-justice system.

Established in 1980, the Norwegian Correctional Service (NCS) is a national-level governmental agency responsible for the execution of all criminal sentences and pretrial detentions in Norway. Its first decade was characterized by multiple challenges. NCS has, as most other correctional systems do, an overarching goal of preventing recidivism. But this task requires a targeted effort against the factors that, according to Norwegian and international research, provide an increased risk of relapse.

Research center for reoffending studies

The Center for Reoffending Studies was established in 2017 by the research department at the University College of Norwegian Correctional Service (KRUS). The aim was to make research on recidivism in the correctional system in Norway visible and easily accessible.

Researcher Ragnar Kristoffersen at KRUS provides updated statistics on recidivism among those who are released from prison and detention sentences, where recidivism includes both custodial and noncustodial sentences for new offences. "Recidivism is defined and measured differently, and this obviously creates a problem when comparing national reoffending rates between nations. A lot of the reported national variation in reoffending rates can be explained by differences in the way recidivism is defined and measured."[3]

According to Kristoffersen, relapse is defined as the first offence date after the release that leads to a new sentence that is to be carried out in the correctional system regardless of the form of

DOI: 10.4324/9781003195887-8

execution. Kristoffersen shows a relatively sharp decline in recidivism among new criminals – those who were released from prison in the years 2017 and 2018 – compared with previous years.[4]

In 2022, Kristoffersen published a report on recidivism among persons released from prison in Norway from 2015–2018.[5] He states that out of 5,023 prisoners released in 2015, 24% were reconvicted, and only 18% of the total of 4,509 released in 2018 returned to prison. This number is even lower than the number reported in the Nordic "Return" report,[6] where the Norwegian recidivism rate was found to be 20% during the first two years after release.[7] This relatively low figure received a lot of international attention and has for many years been used politically to substantiate the direction in the Norwegian prison service. When this report was published in 2010, the former minister of Justice Knut Storberget announced that the report "gives the green light to intensify current criminal policy."

Reading the official recidivism-rate statistics, it seems like there has been a reduction in the recidivism rate over the past 30 years. As we have seen in Storberget's White Paper 37, he focused on the fact that reducing relapses into crime is a shared responsibility across several sectors and levels of administration. NCS, the cooperative agencies, and the municipalities must therefore better coordinate their instruments and make it possible for the convicted person to make their own efforts to change their criminal behavioral patterns. Combined with the focus on values and competence development for prison officers in White Paper 27, this seems to have been a successful formula that has contributed to good results for NCS. The measures in the government's national strategy for 2017–2021 were primarily about closing the remaining gap between prisons and society, so that prisoners can live a future life without committing new crimes. Some measures includes all convicts, regardless of where the sentence is carried out. The strategy is used primarily by employees in the prison service and related staff.

Pick a number?

A challenge for comparative recidivism research internationally is that recidivism is measured in widely disparate ways in different contexts. One of the Norwegian researchers who has specialized in measuring recidivism is Synøve Nygaard Andersen from the University of Oslo.

Andersen's work has highlighted that there is no "correct" or "real" number of relapses, and that what one finds will be greatly influenced by choices related to data and measurement procedures. For instance, reviews of existing research on relapse (see, for example, Armstrong & McNeill, 2012; Harris et al., 2009)[8] show that there are at least five different factors that lead to variations in the results. These include how the selection of offenders is put together, how we define recidivism, how long the follow-up period is, the cultural context of the study, and whether the analysis controls for differences in the personal characteristics of the offenders. In sum, this means we can expect different outcomes from research in this field – just because recidivism is measured in different ways.

Together with Torbjørn Skardhamar, also from the University of Oslo, Andersen has published the article "Pick a number: Mapping recidivism measures and their consequences."[9] Here, the two researchers exploited the richness and flexibility of Norwegian registry data to examine how much national recidivism rates may be affected by how, among whom, and how long recidivism is measured. The paper was published in 2017, and the two authors show that the recidivism rate in Norway varies from 9% to 55% depending on how the repeat offenders among the offenders are grouped and analyzed. Andersen and Skardhamar argue that it is important to read the official Norwegian recidivism research with this in mind.

According to Andersen and Skardhamar, the most cited recidivism rate from Norway by scholars, politicians and media is that of Graunbøl et al (2010).[10] This study reported a Norwegian recidivism rate of 20%, which has received international attention as one of the lowest in Europe – and even in the world (cf. Deady, 2014; Jilani, 2011; Ward, 2013).[11] Andersen and Skardhamar argue that this study solidified the overall impression of Norway – along with the other Nordic countries – as having a progressive, humanitarian, and effective criminal-justice system with low rates of crime, imprisonment, and recidivism (Bondeson, 2005; Deady, 2014; Pratt, 2008; Pratt & Eriksson, 2013; Ward, 2013).[12]

Andersen and Skardhamar say that there are two main limitations to keep in mind when generalizing the recidivism rate of 20% to an international context. Firstly, the Norwegian criminal-justice system has some unique features that could drive these numbers downward. Among them is that Norway imposes imprisonment and other serious sanctions on traffic offenders, who are a particularly low-risk group in terms of reoffending. This and related practices mean that the total recidivism rates are deflated. Secondly, the researchers also remind us that Statistics Norway reports annual recidivism rates, which have remained relatively stable at about 60% (cf. Statistics Norway, 2014; Thorsen et al., 2009).[13] While these numbers are measured differently from those of Graunbøl and colleagues, and while a recidivism rate of 60% might be considered moderate in an international perspective, this nonetheless emphasizes – yet again – that measurement is crucial and that Norwegian exceptionalism might be more nuanced.

Notes

1. Pratt, J. (2008, March). Scandinavian exceptionalism in an era of penal excess: Part I: The nature and roots of Scandinavian exceptionalism. *The British Journal of Criminology, 48*(2), 119–137. https://doi.org/10.1093/bjc/azm072; Pratt, J. (2008, May). Scandinavian exceptionalism in an era of penal excess: Part II: Does Scandinavian exceptionalism have a future? *The British Journal of Criminology, 48*(3), 275–292. https://doi.org/10.1093/bjc/azm073
2. Andersen, S. N., & Skardhamar, T. (2017). Pick a number: Mapping recidivism measures and their consequences. *Crime & Delinquency, 63*(5), 613–635. https://doi.org/10.1177/0011128715570629; Blumstein, A., & Larson, R. C. (1971). Problems in modeling and measuring recidivism. *Journal of Research in Crime and Delinquency, 8*(2), 124–132. https://doi.org/10.1177/002242787100800202; Maltz, Michael D. ([1984] 2001). *Recidivism.* Orlando, Florida: Academic Press, Inc., Originally published. Internet edition available at http://www.uic.edu/depts/lib/forr/pdf/crimjust/recidivism.pdf.
3. The case of Norway.pdf (tilbakefall.no).
4. retur.pdf (unit.no).
5. Kristoffersen, R. (2022). Correctional Statistics of Denmark, Finland, Iceland, Norway and Sweden 2016–2020, University College of Norwegian Correctional Service, **tabell 11** Correctional statistics (unit.no).
6. retur.pdf (unit.no).
7. Denny, M. (2016). Norway's prison system: Investigating recidivism and reintegration. *Bridges: A Journal of Student Research, 10*(10), Article 2. https://digitalcommons.coastal.edu/bridges/vol10/iss10/2
8. Armstrong, S., & McNeill, F. (2012). *Reducing reoffending: Review of selected countries.* SCCJR Research Report No. 04/2012. Glasgow: Scottish Centre for Crime and Justice Research; Harris, P. W., Lockwood, B., & Mengers, L. (2009). Defining and measuring Recidivism. CJCA White paper. Available online from http://www.cjca.net.
9. Andersen & Skardhamar, Pick a Number.
10. Graunbøl, H. M., Kielsrup, B., Muiluvuori, M-L., Tyni, S., Baldurson, E. S., Guðmundsdóttir, H., Kristoffersen, R., Krantz, L., & Lindstén, K. (2010). *Retur. En nordisk undersøgelse af recidiv i kriminalforsorgen* [Return: A Nordic Study of Recidivism Among Clients in the Correctional Service]. Oslo: KRUS
11. Deady, C. W. (2014). Incarceration and Recidivism: Lessons from Abroad. Pell Center for International Relations and Public Policy; Jilani, Z. (2011). As the right bemoans Norway's criminal justice system, it is one of the safest countries on earth. *ThinkProgress;* Ward, T. (2013). Addressing the dual relationship problem in forensic and correctional practice. *Aggression and Violent Behavior, 18,* 92–100.
12. Bondeson, Ulla V. (2005). Crime and criminal in nordic countries. *Society, 42,* 62–70; Deady, C. W. (2014). Incarceration and Recidivism: Lessons from Abroad. Pell Center for International Relations and Public Policy; Pratt, John. (2008, May). Scandinavian exceptionalism in an era of penal excess: Part II: Does Scandinavian exceptionalism have a future? *The British Journal of Criminology, 48*(3), 275–292. https://doi.org/10.1093/bjc/azm073; Pratt, J., & Eriksson, A. (2013). Contrasts in punishment: An explanation of Anglophone excess and Nordic exceptionalism. Routledge; Ward, T. (2013). Addressing the dual relationship problem in forensic and correctional practice. *Aggression and Violent Behavior, 18,* 92–100.
13. Thorsen, L. R., Lid, S., & Stene, R. J. (2009). *Kriminalitet og rettsvesen 2009* [Criminality and the legal system 2009]. Statistical Analyses, 110. Oslo: Statistics Norway.

9

THE HISTORY OF THE NORWEGIAN CORRECTIONAL SYSTEM

At the beginning of the 1700s, penalties with incarceration were uncommon. Physical punishment like branding, whipping and other forms of torture were quite typical. Lifelong labor was also used quite often. After a time, physical punishment was changed to punishment with physical restrictions. In low-security prisons, women were taught household chores while men were trained in trades. At this time slavery was common. Slaves worked in the forts and in the cities. The prisons' double role as an institution for criminals ended with the law on penitentiaries in 1848.

The commission on penal institutions of 1837 concluded that the institutions were completely useless. The commission presented its recommendation in 1841. After the parliament had considered the commission's recommendation and given funds for the establishment of a penitentiary in Christiana (Oslo), construction started in 1844. In 1851 the institution began to be used. The goal of the penitentiary was the effective isolation of the prisoners. The idea was that prisoners should go through a religious cleansing process. Penitentiaries were seen as an improvement, but because of strict isolation, physical discipline was not possible. The demand for isolation meant that prisoners were restricted to simple work in their cells. Prisoners under 35 were expected to have teaching in Norwegian, writing and reading. This was better than out in society.

Prison boards were established in 1875 and so were the regulations. These regulations covered food, clothing, the care of cells, training and discipline. Examples of rewards for good behavior were the opportunity to borrow books, letter-writing privileges, extra food, or extra tobacco. The penitentiary had its own system for classes and rewards. This was dependent on the behavior of the prisoner while he was serving his sentence. In the course of the 1890s, isolation was eased. Still, work training was difficult within the prevailing conditions.

Crowding in prisons and smaller institutions was acute in the 1920s because a number of prisons had been closed at the turn of the century. To ease this situation, in 1933 the parliament decided to buy the Actiebyrggeris lot in Oslo, which bordered on the penitentiary, and to build a new prison there. In 1951 the Prison Reform Committee recommended that the penitentiary should be modernized and the capacity reduced from 226 to 180. When the new law on prisons was discussed and adopted in 1958, the committee placed main emphasis on collectivism in both working conditions and in free time. The removal of freedom of movement was considered a punishment enough in itself. Focus was placed on returning to society. Better possibilities for training in working conditions and hobbies were granted. Leave and limited freedom were given as well. Importantly, a new model was instituted in which different institutions in society give services to the inmates in prison

DOI: 10.4324/9781003195887-9

in the same way that these are given to society outside prisons. Examples of this are health services, school and training, social services, libraries and church services. The Reform Committee also decided to establish a national prison in Trondheim and one close to Oslo. It turned out that it would be too expensive to modernize the main penitentiary so a new national prison in eastern Norway (Ullersmo) should replace that. For financial reasons, only the prison in eastern Norway was built. However, in the 1970s there was a large interior modernization of the national penitentiary.

The Norwegian Association for Criminal Reform (KROM)

1968 is a special year in cultural history, known principally for student protests all over the world. In Norway, the effects of 1968 came first in the beginning of the 1970s. However, in 1968 the Norwegian Association for Criminal Reform was established with a study in legal sociology at the University of Oslo with Thomas Mathiesen as a central figure. This study gave the basic knowledge of central legal institutions and about the court and how the system works. The movement was mostly composed of left-wing forces, and the central idea was that the larger society was the cause of the problems – also those of criminality – not the individual. KROM meant that certain sides of society contributed to the production of crime-producing factors, for example class differences. The first conference was held the next year. The theme was "alternatives to prison." Prison leaders, legal bureaucrats and prisoners participated. The association had a goal that 15% of participants should be prisoners. KROM, with its humanistic and ideological point of view, was critical to the established penal system in Norway. There is no doubt that penal authorities had to give attention to those ideas which KROM stood for. KROM is unique and exists today with yearly conferences.

Challenges in the 1980s

The 1980s were characterized by several challenges for the Norwegian penal system. For example, a large study of repeat offenders carried out by the national institution for statistics, which studied prisoners five years after release, showed that 63% were sentenced again five years after their release. For persons with three or more earlier sentences, the repetition rate was close to 70%. The result of this fact was that politicians were not satisfied and saw the need for a major reform in the penal system. But it wasn't only the incident of repeated crime which was a headache for the relevant authorities. Violence, uneasiness and spectacular prison breaks often characterized the prison environment in the 80s. For example, there was a major revolt in the Oslo Penitentiary in 1984. After this revolt, the Minister of Justice informed the parliament "on conditions in Oslo Penitentiary." After having pointed out "too much isolation," "too little time together," "a lack of sufficient training," old buildings and crowding, it was decided to commission a total analysis of the largest prison in Norway. The debate in Parliament pointed out that prison conditions must be better, occupational training must be significantly increased, along with training services and free-time activities – in other words a strong increase in different forms of collectivism. It wasn't just Oslo Penitentiary that suffered from old and unmodern buildings. Many prisons in the whole country were very old and unmodern with isolation and little activity for the prisoners.

In 1987, a total of 27 prisoners escaped from Oslo Penitentiary, and 13 attempted escapes were registered. Other significant challenges were the sickness HIV (AIDS) and hepatitis. Drug problems increased markedly in the 80s and the percentage of seriously ill prisoners increased after a controversial hospital for serious psychiatric patients (Reitgjerdet) was closed because of undesirable conditions. In 1987, a female prison officer was killed in Ila Prison when she was accompanying a prisoner. In 1991, another prison officer was killed in Sarpsborg Prison.

30 The history of the Norwegian correctional system

The development of crime in the 1980s was also characterized by changes. Drug use had become a large problem in general society, and this development was also reflected in the prison environment. Drug use increased within prisons and organized crime became more common. All these factors brought about a significant retrenchment in regulations at the end of the 80s. The consequence for prisoners was that their days became more limited. In 1988, new laws were established which said that:

1. The key to punishment in prison was the deprivation of freedom of movement
2. Security in and outside the prison should be given the highest priority
3. It is necessary to fight the drug problem in prison.

Differentiation was a key word in this context. Trial release, permissions, the opportunity to tell his own version, etc., should to a higher degree than earlier be a reward for the prisoner who showed that he was motivated to stop criminal behavior.

After being approved in Parliament, these changes in the law brought about an increase of security measures within the prisons. The number of employees was increased based upon a significant rise in crime with increased violence, which led to more organization. There was an increasing number of prisoners with long sentences for violence and drugs in addition to a growing number of prisoners with serious mental sickness.

Until the 80s, the officer's role was connected to traditional security service. There were others who worked with the more positive sides in the prison, such as social workers, teachers, nurses, etc. For prison officers, this meant that their role was solely as officers and there was little positive interaction between warders and prisoners. Working together was considered negative since there was a basic mistrust between warders and prisoners. This brought about unfortunate incidents of uneasiness and violence. It was an evil circle.

Why is the correctional service of Norway so humane?

Harald Føsker, former director, has his own thoughts on why the Norwegian correctional service is humane.

"Before World War II in Norway, many politicians were imprisoned for military denial or sedition. During the war, several of them were also placed at Grini, a German concentration camp in Oslo run by the German occupiers. One of the former prisoners at Grini, Einar Gerhardsen, was prisoned three times during the war. After the war, he became Prime Minister in Norway from 1945 to 1951. He also was Prime Minister from 1955 to 1965 and was later referred to as 'the Father of the country.'

Harald Føsker remembers that Gerhardsen made a strong impression on the student prison officers when he visited the University College of Norwegian Correctional Service (KRUS) in the 80's.

"We invited Gerhardsen to a student prison officer evening in 1980 where he was to tell us about his life as a prisoner. He told us that this experience from three different institutions; Oslos main police station Møllergata 19, Grini and the concentration camp Sachsenhausen changed his view of the prison officer.

He told us about the huge contrast between the nice people who worked in the Norwegian prison system and the "pigs" who worked for the Nazis in the other two prisons.[1]

"I believe that to understand the present it is necessary to know the past. The understanding of the present is the key to active participation in the future. Historical knowledge and insight form a platform for identifying processes both in society and corrections," Føsker says. He believes that the humane correctional practice started already in the 50s with the Prison Act of 1952 and 1958, which is very puritanical and treatment-oriented. Føsker believes that the later humane prison reforms and humane politicians were formed by the attitude of the politicians who later ruled the country, who had themselves been subjected to imprisonment, and that affected the parliamentary majority.

Without the generation of politicians who were imprisoned, he believe the penal care system would not have been so humane. He also says that it is important to understand the context at the time when the prisons in Norway were built. Among other things, Botsen was built in such a way that it would meet special challenges and was used as a replacement for the fortress prisons, especially in Akershus. The prison authorities at the time looked to the US and built Botsen in 1851 according to the Philadelphia model. It was inspired by a former prison in Pennsylvania called the Eastern State Penitentiary that was operational until 1971. The building of the prison was the largest and most expensive public structure ever erected in the United States and quickly became a model for more than 300 prisons worldwide.

In Norway, the politicians wanted to build seven prisons like this, but this is the only one due to lack of money.

Interview with most dangerous man Arne Treholt[2]:

There were shock waves flowing through public debates when former official politician Arne Treholt (born in 1942) was arrested on a plane just before taking off on January 20th, 1984, and charged for espionage.

The day Treholt was arrested he was the spokesman of the Norwegian Ministry of Foreign Affairs. After several months in custody, he was convicted of treason and espionage for the benefit of the Soviet Union and Iraq. Treholt declared himself not guilty of the charge of espionage and has never admitted guilt or having handed over material that could have damaged Norwegian interests to a foreign country, but when the verdict fell, he got a sentence of 20 years in prison. When he was imprisoned, Treholt was considered one of the most dangerous men in Norway. This also affected his three imprisonments in Drammen (19 months), in department K in Ila (12 months) and in Ullersmo Prison in Oslo where he served his time in prison until he was released for health reasons in 1992.

We wanted to hear about the experiences Treholt had after his 102 months as a prisoner, so we visited him.

"Pastry. Bring some pastry for the coffee," he says on the telephone a short time before our first meeting. And his striking blue eyes lighten up when we come with pastry from the local bakery in Oslo, the capital of Norway. Even if he is almost 80 years old, it is easy to recognize the eager man with his white hair and smiling eyes. The former marathon runner is obviously in good physical condition and runs before us up the stairs to the flat where we have agreed to meet.

It was when he was affiliated with the Norwegian UN delegation in New York as embassy councilor and later as council chief in the Foreign Ministry's press department that he became interested in long-distance running. This was a passion it was difficult to maintain when he was behind bars, but even in captivity he tried to exercise physically at least one hour every day, running around the little "box" at the top of the prison, seven meters round and round for one hour every day.

"The physical exercise, writing and reading saved me," he says thoughtfully and carefully. Treholt has had a long and impressive professional career as a journalist, a member of the Labor Party, political secretary and Deputy minister in the secretariat which worked for the establishment of a Norwegian 200-mile economic zone while he was in the Ministry of Foreign Affairs, and as a diplomat in the Norwegian Foreign Service before the fatal day when he was arrested. Since he was released from prison he has been living abroad, but we meet him in Oslo, where he stays with a family member, in December 2021 to talk about his experiences with the Norwegian prison service. The tough experiences behind bars have given him a broad perspective, but he clarifies that he is not bitter, nor does he carry any resentments against anyone.

PHOTO 9.1 Convicted spy Arne Treholt in Ila Prison where he served several years
Source: Photo: Vidar Ruud, Arbark

You were considered a "dangerous prisoner," especially after your escape attempt from Ila. How were you treated by the prison officers?

"At first, I will say that those who work in Norwegian prison service are well-educated and do the best they can, but it is not that easy when the system is so rigid. Norway is still criticized for letting people stay in custody far too long. I, myself, was isolated for 19 months before I got the verdict," he says and admits that the first months were depressing. When he was working in the UN system, he, himself, had the responsibility for social issues and was often involved in interrogations about the judiciary conditions in countries with which Norway does not like to compare itself. He says,

> When I suddenly ended up behind bars in Norway, I realized that there was a great distance between words spoken about our prison care and how it really was. After I was arrested, I was put in a room without a window for two months at the police station in Oslo. I was still in a state of shock after the arrest and the long questionings were exhausting. In addition, I did not know whether it was day or night and I slept very little. Even when I had to use the toilet the prison officers went there too and I felt very vulnerable.

"I understood it was done so to make me confess and that was an enormous strain. Perhaps this practice is changed, but for me it was extremely tough," he says. He was transferred to Drammen Prison, which is a unit with a high security level. This prison has an ordinary capacity of 54 male prisoners. The prison prioritizes inmates with custody sentence or people with short sentences. Treholt tells us he was put in solitary confinement, was not allowed to use any media, or have visitors. Dark curtains in front of the window meant that he didn't know the difference between night and day: a part of the psychological terror he endured in custody. His prison cell was placed next to the elevator shaft and every time the elevator stopped it was like someone gave him a blow to the head.

> I survived because I was disciplined and made myself my own fixed habits. I put my honor in having got out of bed when the inspection came at 7 a.m. and fully used the hour when I was out, even if it was a rather small space, and the roof was covered with steel mesh. There I ran around in the tiny space letting myself dream of running a marathon. When you are imprisoned, you must engage yourself in small fantasy exercises. In my case, I was never offered work training or studies because that was considered too dangerous. When I was taken to interrogation all the corridors were cleared so that I should have no contact with other prisoners due to the presumed sensitivity of the case.

This later led to myths about him being a dangerous prisoner.

After the trial he waited six weeks before he got the verdict and during that time, he experienced something that made a great impression on him.

> It was a terrible time when I sat boiling in my own insecurity, and then I suddenly got a visitor in the cell. The head of the prison board, Georg Rieber Mohn, went in. He told me he himself got claustrophobia so he could understand this was hard for me. He also told me he knew I loved running and asked me if I would care for a treadmill in my tiny little air yard. I certainly would! I got the treadmill, and even a rib wall from the cellar, so I got two fine training posts for my free air hour. I wore out many pairs of sneakers and ran 15 kilometres in an hour. On Sundays we got two hours in fresh air. I was asked if I wanted to be a training coach for fellow prisoners who were young boys. Some as young as 13–14 years. It surprised me that a so-called humane prison system undertook to keep minors locked in isolation in a breach of international conventions Norway has signed. I as a representative for the Norwegian government had criticised other countries for violating these conventions in the United Nations.

I agreed and in companionship with the prison doctor I was their coach for many weeks as I waited for the verdict. These youngsters were in prison on short term for having smoked hash or used heavier stuff. It shocked me to watch how we in Norway treated children in prison and I talked much about this in the press. I knew that many people in the government and both the Minister of Justice and the Minister of Social Affairs responded to this, so some changes were made.

"If I shall sum up my first years in police houses and in custody in Drammen, I would say these are things the Norwegian authorities don't need to be proud of." Treholt also remembers he had to take off all his clothes in a small room crowded with people when he arrived in Drammen Prison.

You have in your books criticized the system more than the prison officers – can you elaborate what is wrong with the system?

He says,

> My purpose, why I wanted to write down my experiences was to try to point to the nuances in the situation. I met a lot of good well-educated prison officers who respected us and treated us kindly, but it is the organization of the system that does not work. As I saw it there was a long distance between they who took the decisions and the employees who worked with us. Instead of being able to have influence on their own working situation and the prisoners' conditions of imprisonment they always had to carry out orders from people higher up in the system.

When Treholt was transferred to Ila Prison, he was first put in Department K, mostly populated with prisoners with enormous mental disorders who had been patients in restrained departments in Reitgjerdet hospital when this hospital was closed.

"That I was placed in the same department as people with mental disorders was another shock and a huge burden. Every day people came from the hospital department with drug boards loaded with medicines and syringes for my fellow prisoners.

> Department K is a variant of the famous film *One Flew Over the Cuckoo's Nest*. Three times a day we were locked out of our cells. When I should eat breakfast, it used to be just me in the

PHOTO 9.2 Arne Treholt in December 2021

Source: Photo: Alf Ragnar Olsen

kitchen since the others still slept. But at lunch about twelve o'clock I always had to make sure I was placed with my back to the wall. At that time everything could happen. At first, I did not understand why the cutting knife was curly. But gradually I learned there were many incidents. One of the imprisoned was originally an engineer who had fallen down a stair to a plane and suffered brain damaged. Sometimes he smeared himself with his own excrement before he came to join us for lunch. I certainly understood what had happened, but not all the others did.

You were imprisoned when there was a lot of turbulence in the prison-care system, among other things, in 1988 when a female prison officer at Ila was killed. The regime was tightened – what consequences did that have upon your own imprisonment?

I consider that murder a disastrous mistake from the prison authorities because the man who killed her had threatened to do this many times, and he was a strong man. He lifted 150-kilo weights in the fitness room, and he boasted that the young officer was his and that he would beat us up if we talked to his "girl". Letting him go to the cinema alone with this officer was a fatal decision. She was killed and we all got extra punishment.

"I was denied leaving the prison for any social event and so it was for six and a half year. A very long time," he says. The murder of the prison officer and the escape of a Swedish prisoner who was convicted for espionage resulted in panic and hysteria.

And we, the other imprisoned, had to pay the price. We got extra punishment even if we had nothing to do with it. I felt it was a shame to experience this and that it was against all international rules. The planned escape attempt was to a change in my existence so that I could keep my identity and make an end to the nightmare I was in. It was hysteria connected to the attempt someone had whispered about my planned escape before I could make it happen.

He says quietly,

I had been interviewed by some media where I could talk about everything except my own case, so an officer always listened to the conversations. It felt kind of special to walk with handcuffs through the corridors and through 15 doors that were unlocked and locked again when I was to meet someone. Luckily, my father could visit me at Ila Prison so that was the bright spot in my existence. My dad came at exactly ten o'clock every Saturday. That meant everything to me.

Treholt also remembers there were more narcotics in the prison which meant that the control regime was changed, and all the prisoners were examined for narcotics from time to time.

I felt that extremely troublesome after having family visitors, visit from a lawyer or others stopping by. During one single day it happened I had to strip to my skin 3 or 4 times even if everyone knew I had never touched narcotics. Everybody had to be checked and that was the reason why they could intervene in our physical integrity. Once after a training session on a bicycle I burst with anger when I was commanded to take off my clothes. I threw my underpants in the officer's face and got internal punishment and denial of leave because the situation was seen as if I had threatened him and then the result is collective punishment.

The escape attempt was the reason why Treholt was transferred to Ullersmo Prison, and even here he was put in solitary confinement, but he was let out and back in three times a day.

He says,

> We were about five to six persons in the same department and what differed from Ila was that we were allowed to sit together in a common area for two hours during the evening. But a year should pass before I was let out into the community of an ordinary department. By then I had been kept in isolation for four years. One thing I regret is that I let photographers and journalist come into my cell. They took photos of me sitting in front of the TV as if I had a wonderful time. But everyone who has experienced being kept inside four walls and a roof for years knows that this is extremely hard. I can almost call it torture.

The myths

When he was transferred to Ullersmo, there was an official debate whether they should have a plane- and helicopter-free zone over the prison.
Shaking his head, he says,

> Later I saw that the myths about how dangerous I was were totally crazy. Then I became aware of that the authorities had supervised me and my family 24/7 for seven to eight years before I was arrested. When they did not find anything interesting their fantasies about me became the strangest myths.

There are a lot of fine terms in Norwegian prison care like contact-officer scheme, dynamic safety, the principle of subsidiarity, social representations, rehabilitation, etc. – do these words comply with how you perceived reality?

He shakes his head and even his whole body.

> Who the hell knows what this means? I think we must look to the practice and to the international regulations and not adorn us with fine words. But it is not that simple to change a system. Then the decision makers must understand what's going on in a prison.

Treholt believes there are no big differences between the justice policy by different governments. "We who are imprisoned notice no difference. Perhaps they from the labor movement have a bit softer attitude but unfortunately what concerns prison and imprisonment are controlled by the opinions made outside in the society."

How was the prison community?

"As I have told it sometimes was demanding. But when I came to Ullersmo I tried to help if someone asked me. At the most I wrote 35–40 applications for other prisoners, and it became a common joke that 'this is a real Treholt application,'" he tells with a smile. Life experiences from prison have influenced all the decisions he has taken since then. And still in prison he met another prisoner who he married. But even she found the regime strict when he got his leave. 15 police officers were on guard when they had dinner with friends.

"I will once again say that it is not the individual who is the problem but the system," he says.

Does Norway have any reason to boast of having "the best prison care in the world"?

"I think I am not the right man to answer this question," Arne Treholt says smiling, "but I am not impressed."

It is now more than 60 years since the book *The Society of Captives*[3] written by the American criminologist Greham Sykes was published in 1958. Maybe this is one of the most important books in criminology because he attempted to find out the extent to which prisons can succeed in their attempts to control every facet of life – or whether the strong bonds between prisoners make it impossible to run a prison without finding ways of "accommodating" the prisoners.

But as the years have passed there is still a lot of prison pain, also in Norwegian prisons according to researchers. We have already heard the story of the former inmate Arne Treholt who served time in the 80s. But even today there are prisoners struggling with multiple health problems. In a book that was published in 2021, Mette Irmgard Snertingdal (2021, p. 188) wrote that "even if Norwegian prisoners do not lose their civil rights, prison pain is still a current issue in Norwegian prisons as well," something she herself believes should worry employees in the Norwegian prison service far more. In her closing remark she writes that it is important that this insight about prison pain among Norwegian prisoners should not be diminished, concealed, or repressed. She encourages people in the prison service not to obscure the importance of humane prisoner treatment from prisoners' perspectives on the execution of sentences (Snertingdal & Nymo, 2021).[4] A recent survey shows that inmates in Norwegian prisons experience an increased need for care. Prison and health service employees report that inmates have more extensive mental disorders, somatic diseases, and age-related disorders now than before.

Notes

1. Personal communication with Harald Føsker 2022.
2. Arne Treholt, personal communication: December 15, 2021 in Oslo.
3. The Society of Captives – Gresham M. Sykes – pocketbook (9780691130644) | Adlibris Bokhandel.
4. Snertingdal, M., & Nymo, K. (2021). *Jeg skal bli fengselsbetjent*. Fagbokforlaget.

10
HALDEN PRISON: PUNISHMENT THAT WORKS – CHANGE THAT LASTS!

There is a growing global interest in Scandinavian incarceration, and especially Halden Prison in Norway. Every week there are visitors from abroad coming to the prison close to the Swedish border. Halden Prison has been the subject of multiple feature stories in British and American media, TV series and newspaper articles. Michael Moore also profiled this prison in one of his recent movies.[1] During a visit to Halden Prison, the former UK MP Ann Widdecombe[2] fronted in a TV program an insight into a whole new, modern model of rehabilitation trialed in Norway.

But what is the regime and operation of the prison and the underlying philosophies that make this prison distinctive?

Are Høidal gives us the history of Halden:

Halden has been a prison town for hundreds of years.

Construction started on Fredriksten fortress in 1661 and was finished ten years later. In 1682 they decided to extend it, and the work that was completed in 1700 made the fortress look much as it does today. From 1665 onwards, convicts sentenced to penal servitude served their terms in Fredriksten fortress' slave hold. In the early 1800s, up to 200 slaves were held at the fortress. This practice continued until 1845, when the slave hold was closed, and the remaining convicts were transferred to Fredrikstad fortress.

In 1841, the Penal Establishment Commission published their review of prison conditions in Norway. The findings were not good. Most prisoners were held in either fortresses or workhouses, and the commission was highly critical of the conditions. In the Norwegian Parliamentary Select Committee Report, NOU 1984:2, entitled "Education for Employment in Correctional Services," prison conditions are described as follows:

> Prisoners in the fortresses were shackled in irons, and with the exception of those who were at work, the prisoners were kept in large common areas, day and night. Prisoners, shackled in irons, walking the streets on their way to and from work, were a common sight in the fortress towns.

Halden was one such fortress town, and in Fredriksten conditions were exactly as described by the commission.

The select committee report further states:

> The Commission concluded that the establishments were completely inappropriate, nor were they sufficiently deterrent, especially as the unimpeded fraternization between inmates was

DOI: 10.4324/9781003195887-10

further from an improving influence than to constitute schooling in criminality. The committee recommended a total reform of the system, with fortresses and slave holds to be closed down and replaced with purpose-built prisons containing cells, where inmates could be held separately, day and night, and undergo a religious purifying process.

In the years that followed, an historic development of prisons throughout the whole of Norway was set in motion. The main penitentiary in Christiania (Oslo) was the first to be completed, housing up to 240 inmates. During the following decade, 56 local prisons were built. In Halden, Fredrikshald District Prison was opened in 1863/1864. Similar district prisons were built in the nearby towns Moss, Sarpsborg, Fredrikstad and Eidsberg at around the same time.

The prevailing philosophy of the time was that isolation would change prisoners' mindsets. Inmates should remain alone to think about what they had done. They were therefore held in continuous isolation 24 hours a day. This philosophy of isolation continued until the Prison Reform Committee of 1951 did a complete reversal, and instead placed emphasis on communal employment and free time. The committee also stated that detention in itself was punishment enough. This 1951 committee established the small beginnings of today's philosophy in the Norwegian Correctional Service, which has advanced over the years with Minister for Justice Inger Louise Valle's (Labor Party) White Paper on Criminality of the 1970s, and onward to the government white papers of 1997 and 2007.

Valle became justice minister in 1973 and held the position for six years. No other Minister of Justice has had as much influence on penal politics than she did. However, when she presented her point of view on the most possibly humane penal system in the Message to Parliament from 1978, she received a great deal of opposition from the entire political spectrum, including her own party. Those opposed to her claimed that she made life too easy for prisoners. The debate on the message from Valle was hard. Media was also hard on Valle both as a person and on her rudimentary attitude. Today almost everything in the Message to parliament has been instituted. Possibly the most important of these came some years later when the penal system with open sentences was established.

> Open sentences include all help and control efforts which are used in correctional trial situations: for example trial freedom and rules of law with a restricted sentence. Yes, trial freedom can be used as a joint name for organized work with prisoners outside the prison.
>
> In 1959, there was only one full-time teaching post for the entire Norwegian Correctional Service. By 1979 this figure had risen to around 100. The 1970s were a time of significant change in terms of opportunities for inmates.

Fredrikshald District Prison eventually became Halden Local Prison. It remained in operation for 110 years, closing in 1974. New prisons were built in both Moss and Sarpsborg, while Fredrikstad Prison remained operational until the new Halden Prison was opened in 2010. The old Eidsberg Prison is still in use, as part of the new "Inner Østfold Prison."

A paradigm shift

The 80s and early 90s were a challenging period for the Norwegian Correctional Service (NCS), with hostile climates inside of prisons for staff and inmates, many negative incidents, and increased public concern about the waiting list for serving sentences that had built up during this period. There was, in other words, a significant need to push NCS in a new direction. A significant effort was therefore initiated by the new director of NCS to develop a new framework for Norwegian corrections. The focus was to channel the available resources toward a more targeted, goal-oriented correctional service. The many goals for this effort included:

1. Reducing recidivism
2. Improving the professionalism of NCS and officers during the execution of sentences
3. Developing new methods for supervising, rehabilitating, and working with inmates
4. Implementing organizational and administrative changes that would enable officers to work more actively and directly with inmates, in order to make meaningful changes in their lives.

Pursuing these goals was a practically and philosophically complicated and sensitive process. Therefore, it was politically necessary to document the proposed direction of NCS in a parliamentary report. The result was White Paper no. 27 (1997–1998) about NCS (hereafter "White Paper I"). Although this might sound both dry and bureaucratic, White Paper I signaled a transformative moment in the modern history of Norwegian corrections. White Paper I – and its chapter on values, principles, main objectives, and performance goals in particular – generally determined the direction of NCS for the years to come. The set of policy and philosophical goals outlined in the document marked a paradigm shift for Norwegian corrections and remains the foundation for today's NCS. As a direct consequence of this new set of basic norms and principles, the approach to corrections was radically changed, and prison officers were given a much greater responsibility for the rehabilitation of inmates, not just their incarceration. This, in turn, led to a series of necessary changes in the educational requirements for and training of correctional officers. Importantly, White Paper I was also focused on the dual goal of both reducing recidivism and working to reduce the unintended negative consequences of serving a sentence either in prison or in society. White Paper I created a common, cross-political understanding of Norwegian criminal-justice policy and laid the groundwork for the development of the correctional service we have had in place for the past 20 years.

"New Halden Prison"

During the debate in the Parliament on White Paper I, the following point was raised: "The committee are aware that the need for remand and prison places is especially great in Eastern Norway. Based on the need for greater capacity, and the calculations presented in this white paper, the committee would like to propose the following: Parliament asks the government to begin planning work on a new prison in Østfold County."

The choice of Østfold County was certainly due in part to the pressure on prison places in the area, however, this was also an opportunity to close down a number of smaller prisons. Halden Local Prison had already closed in 1974, but it was expected that Moss, Fredrikstad and Sarpsborg would also be decommissioned when the new prison was finished.

Parliament finally gave formal permission for planning of the new prison in Østfold in 1999. This started a political tug-of-war between the towns in Østfold as to who would gain this large, public-sector workplace. The final decision on the site was made in March 2003, and Halden was selected after strong competition from several towns in Østfold. Construction work began in 2006, the foundation stone was laid in the spring of 2008, and Halden Prison opened to inmates on March 1, 2010, with an official opening on April 8th, 2010. The prison has 252 places for male inmates, both remand places and places for those serving a sentence. There are 228 places behind the prison walls, divided between three wings and 24 places in a transitional accommodation block just outside the walls.

The buildings of Halden Prison cover an area of 27,000 square meters, and the walls enclose a total area of 37 acres. The distance between the walls and the surrounding forest, the "unobstructed visibility zone," is the same size. The wall surrounding the prison is 1.4 kilometers long and six meters high.

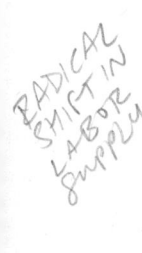

Altogether, employees of the Norwegian Correctional Service and all their collaborating partners in Halden Prison equate to about 350 full-time positions of employment.

As of January 1, 2017, Sarpsborg Prison, with places for 25 inmates, has been incorporated into Halden Prison. As a result, Halden Prison now has a total capacity of 277 places.

Why Halden Prison is special

Halden Prison is renowned for its architecture. The structure is designed to "meet inmates and employees in a friendly and non-authoritarian manner. The design work has therefore focused on good relationships, good dimensions, quality of materials and strength."[3] During the planning phase for Halden Prison, the waiting list for prison places in Norway was quite long.

The new prison was intended to reduce this problem, but there were also higher aims for this establishment. It was to become a flagship prison, showcasing the modern-day Correctional Service. In a pamphlet published in 2007, Secretary of State Terje Moland Pedersen (AP) stated, "I want Halden Prison to be a pioneer within Correctional Services, facilitating good opportunities for offenders to break the cycle of criminality they are in. It will be the most modern prison in Europe."

Alongside the architecture and outside spaces, there is a special building inside the walls which grabs the attention of visitors: the large Activity Centre. Halden Prison was the first prison in Norway (and for the time being, the last) where you can find workplaces, a college, social/employment services, social workers, library services and prison officers together under one roof. This has provided unique opportunities for a new type of interdisciplinary cooperation. Many of the workshops include educational facilities, so the college can provide vocational courses. In addition, the college has its own training venues, where inmates can complete apprenticeships in a number of different disciplines.

PHOTO 10.1 Halden prison in Norway opened in 2010 engages buildings and landscape actively for people in an extreme life situation

Source: Halden prison

The green prison

Correctional services all over the world must have an active relationship with the green shift and the Paris Agreement. There are a lot of possibilities "behind the walls" and in probation. There are many good ideas in the initiative New European Bauhaus and that gives inspiration to think more innovatively in the further development of correctional services.

It is also important to motivate those who are interested to join this green shift. There are many sustainable elements we can focus on in a prison.

Architecture and surroundings

Halden Prison itself architecturally, interior-wise and in the outdoor space, focuses on green and environmental elements. Halden Prison has received much attention because of its architecture. The architects followed this up with the solution of having a divided building that requires a transfer between the various units. This can be said to reflect our everyday movement between home, school, workplaces, etc. (the normality principle). The facility is defined by the idea that high-quality surroundings, connected to nature, can help build self-esteem and respect. The facility is designed "so that it meets the inmates and employees in a friendly, and non-authoritarian way. Therefore, emphasis is placed on good relationships, good dimensions, qualities in material use and strength in the forms." This is in accordance with the principle of normality and that progression through a sentence should be aimed as much as possible at returning to the community. The more closed a system is, the harder it will be to return to freedom. We believe that the level of activity and reintegration efforts is the main reason for the low level of aggression and violence in Halden Prison. Other reasons are the overall good compliance with prison regulations and, based on statements from inmates, that they do appreciate the facilities, the surroundings and the reduced feeling of being in a high-security prison.

The building project is organized by simple volumes placed within a beautiful woodland landscape. The builders have placed an emphasis on using high-quality materials, generous dimensions, openness and light to create an environment that goes against traditional prison design, providing a new perspective on prison architecture. The functions of each building are distinguished by their material selection and connection with the surrounding landscape. Halden Prison is really the green prison physically.

Halden Prison is the first prison in Norway with solar energy

The Norwegian government has given millions in a package of measures to stimulate green change. Climate-friendly solutions such as solar cells are a focus area for Norway. These are measures that benefit both the environment and those who use the buildings. The solar panels must be mounted on accessible roof surfaces. There will be many square meters of solar cells throughout the prison. This is a pilot project in the Norwegian Correctional Service. Other elements Halden prison work with in this green shift are:

1. Reuse of textiles, furniture and other articles. This is sensible work for the inmates
2. Source sorting for a better environment. Can also provide jobs for inmates
3. More use of "green products," like "fair trade products" and organic food.

Retreat – time for reflection in Halden Prison

Retreat means "withdrawal." During the retreat, inmates withdraw from their daily chores for meditation and concentration. Silence and a fixed daily rhythm are the main elements when conducting a retreat. At a retreat, people are silent together. Through four different periods in the long retreat (three or four weeks), they have themes and tasks that provide a good progression in changing tasks. The themes are adapted to the individual's personal plan for participation. Personal guidance from professional supervisors is the mainstay of the entire retreat. But where did we get this idea from?

Swedish project on Kumla Prison

In the year 2000, Kumla Prison in Sweden started up with an initiative they called "monastic activities." In the "monastery," long-term convicts who had not entered the leave scheme could retire and undergo a retreat. This meant that they withdrew from everyday life in prison in a separate retreat ward. Here they could quietly go into themselves, meet themselves "in the depths," deal with previous actions and begin to look ahead to a crime-free life with a good quality of life.

When Norway opened Halden Prison in 2010, the idea quickly came to establish a similar unit for the implementation of retreats. In the prison, the conditions were physically right to create such a ward sheltered from the other units and there was even a beautiful air yard attached to this unit. The first retreat was carried out for two weeks in 2013 with a good reception from the inmates. In 2014, we tried a three-week retreat that was once again well received. Over the years, the offer has been expanded, and in 2022 Halden Prison will conduct a retreat each month with different lengths, from one to four weeks. Prisoners from all over Norway can apply for a retreat in Halden Prison.

Silence and tranquility

Retreats are days of silence for inmates who want to find peace and balance in life. Time is spent concentrating, meditating, and praying. They should go into their own lives and ask themselves the question, "Who am I?" Through tools such as silence, bible texts, meditation/reflection and guidance conversations, the individual inmate will have the opportunity to reflect on what has happened in life, deal with the past and think about what they want for the future. There are tough processes and hard work with oneself. It is important to be motivated for change and create a new course in life. The process is supported by professional supervisors both during the retreat and afterwards. The offer is open to everyone regardless of outlook on life and background. The goal of the retreats is to gain greater self-insight and discover the good in each individual. Furthermore, through participation, it is desired that the individual takes a stand against his or her own past and creates a better self-image. Through the retreat, it is desired that the individual will feel relief and forgiveness for their previous life, make new choices in life and feel that they are helped to live a responsible life after release.

The community with the other participants is very central, even if this takes place in silence. It is an atmosphere of openness, trust and recognition. Going through strong things together gives belonging.

The four themes you work with in the long retreats are:

1. Goodness and love
2. Evil, suffering and the settlement of sin
3. A new start and the life to be lived
4. Hope and opportunities, and the choices that must be made.

According to the management, the results of the retreat in Halden Prison are so far very good. Most people who have been through it since the beginning in 2013 are still doing very well in life. About 95% of them have survived without recidivism.

Notes

1. Norwegian Prison – Michael Moore – YouTube.
2. 'The Seekers' Conversation with former UK MP Ann Widdecombe – YouTube.
3. From Statsbygg's – State Construction's – completion report in 2010 – nr 686/2010.
4. From the final report, Halden prison.

11

TROND GETS A WAKE-UP CALL IN HALDEN PRISON

Trond had never believed that he would change when he entered the gate of Halden Prison. The heroin addict had lost his lust for life and saw no future for himself. But in the drug department, he got a wake-up call that changed everything.

The prison had long been working on plans to open its own substance-abuse unit based on the Canadian program for those struggling with substance abuse when they entered.

The program was called the National Substance Abuse Programme (NSAP)[1] and the goal was to make an individual plan for how people should cope with continuing to be drug-free after release. NSAP was more individually adapted than the old offering and had three different levels of intensity, a clearer link between crime and intoxication, a greater emphasis on problem-solving skills and future planning. To succeed, they also had to work closely with the Norwegian Labor and Welfare Administration (NAV) and the home municipality of the inmate. When Trond was offered to be one of the first to complete the NSAP program, he immediately accepted. The drug addict had actually given up and had a dark vision of the future. But in the addiction department, he got a proper wake-up call that changed everything. "In here I was respected and listened to. It was a different atmosphere that made me safe. We could talk openly about how drugs affected our lives and make individual plans for a drug-free future," he says.

"I was heavily intoxicated when I was out of prison and for me my only thought was often just how to get my next shot," he says. In the department together with others who were struggling with the same substance-abuse problem, they were able to reflect on the advantages and disadvantages of being sober.

"I was grown up and ready for a change and was grateful to have another opportunity through this 12-week sentence option," he says. The 12-week imprisonment alternative is only part of the program.

Life in the substance-abuse unit was the same as in the other units. During the day they worked, and they had over 30 meetings where they talked about intoxication.

> Each one of us wrote down concrete goals for how we envisioned life in ten years. This program saved me and the other day I looked at the file from that time and saw that I had managed all the goals I set myself, except the training target. I probably should have trained more.

DOI: 10.4324/9781003195887-11

PHOTO 11.1 Minister of Justice Knut Storberget greets inmate Trond Henriksen during the opening of the substance-abuse unit in Halden Prison, 2011

Source: Photo: Halden Prison

The most important thing was probably that employees treated him with respect even though he had had major substance-abuse problems. "It is important that people who have struggled with intoxication receive this type of follow-up so that we can get out drug-free and with a brighter future perspective. Many of us were destructive and thought negative thoughts," he says. Trond says the staff were working more socially in this department, motivating the inmates and giving them hope and more self-confidence. "It was a wake-up call. Suddenly I experienced a change and I regained faith in myself. The program gives us the courage to take hold of our own lives and not let intoxication control the future," he says.

Damaged

What was most difficult for Trond as a prisoner was to show emotion. Big boys in prison don't cry. In particular, the 14 months in solitary confinement with mail and restraining orders in Oslo Prison had affected his emotional life. "Not everyone understands how harmful isolation in prison is. It's very devastating to the head and I was scared by my own thoughts when I was isolated," he admits. Specially, there were extremely destructive thoughts about the employees and the management who had locked him up. He says,

> It was awful sitting alone with my own thoughts and this scared me to death. I still have injuries from this. I can't stand crying or showing emotion when other people can see me. Even if I'm touched by something positive, I'll hide if the tears come.

But he knows that the situation for Norwegian inmates has changed, and that people are getting more help today, he says,

> The prison staff in Norway have a fundamental attitude that they treat inmates with respect and so does our entire society. How a society treats people who have ended up outside tells a lot about what kind of society we have, and in that respect, Norway is one of the better ones. Here, among other things, I believe the USA has something to learn from Norwegian correctional services.

After his time in the substance-abuse unit, Trond is transferred to a normal cell.

Second chance as radio host

Trond sits alone in his cell in Halden Prison. Everyone has his own single cell here. It's the nicest cell he's ever had all these years behind bars. There are tiles in the bathroom, a flat-screen TV and dedicated employees who care. The media image created so far about Halden Prison has not realized that being deprived of liberty is one of the worst things that can happen to a person. Trond longs to do something meaningful to get rid of his darkest thoughts. Then there is a knock on the door. In comes the prison officer. "How would you like to start the world's first prisoner radio to go out on the FM band for everyone?" he asks enthusiastically with eager sparkling in his big brown eyes.

Trond looks at him in surprise: "What do you mean?"

The prison manager had had conversations with Radio Prime, which had stations in a Swedish city and in several Norwegian cities in the region. They wanted the station to broadcast an hour of prisoner radio a week.

Trond rises from his bed and looks gratefully at the leader, whom he jokingly calls dad, and gives him a great hug. He finally sees an opportunity to do something meaningful that brings him joy. He accepts the offer to become the world's first editor of prisoner radio on the FM tape. It will air on September 1, 2011. Training with him and three other inmates will start immediately.

Radio on air

Trond has some radio experience from before and soon the first episode is recorded. There's the film about the big Nokas bank robbery to be reviewed and one of the robbers himself is going to roll the dice.[1]

Due to the terror attack on Norway on July 22 the same year (ref Chapter 12 on this), the broadcast is postponed because it also contains shooting scenes. The shooting is edited away, and the film is a dicey 3 by the Nokas robber, because he thinks there is too little love in it.

The inmate radio hosts spend a lot of time on what the broadcasts should contain. Outside the walls there are many myths about life in prison and they want to punch holes in some of them and orientate people on reality. In the broadcasts, they address the criticism of isolation and custody in the Norwegian Correctional Service and other current issues from the inmates' perspective. It becomes a popular radio station that many people listen to. It is hard work and requires full concentration and discipline. Today it is Røverradioen (The Robber Radio) which is based in Oslo. Halden Prison contributes individual entries to these radio broadcasts.

---

1. In Norway, the expression 'roll the dice' is commonly used among the film reviewers and book reviewers when they evaluate a film or book using the numbers from one to six like on the dice.

There are also other programs that the prison offers to former drug addicts, sex offenders and pedophiles. These programs aim to improve their lives to make them ready for life outside. Always remember that the inmate can be your next neighbor.

Today the Norwegian Correctional Service does not use NSAP. The prisons use a Norwegian-composed program called "Er-Vil-Kan."

> "If one man can create that much hate, you can only imagine how much love we as a togetherness can create."
>
> *Stine Renate Håheim to CNN, July 23, 2011, the day after the terror attack*

Note

1. https://krus.brage.unit.no/krus-xmlui/bitstream/handle/11250/160582/Evalueringsrapportpercent20NSAP.pdf?sequence=1&isAllowed=y

12
VIOLENT EXTREMISM, TERRORISM AND RADICALIZATION IN THE PRISONS

July 22, 2011 terror attacks in Norway

Former director of the Directorate and now senior adviser Harald Føsker[1] is on holiday. He's just barely stopped by the office on the fifth floor of the Ministry of Justice when the bomb goes off. A terrorist had placed a car bomb near the high-rise in the middle of Oslo, the block that houses both the prime minister's office and the Ministry of Justice. It's 3:25 p.m. on July 22, 2011. Then the bomb blows! Føsker is thrown backwards by window structures and glass that come towards him with furious speed. Everything turns black!

When after a few minutes he wakes up, he is totally blinded and understands that he is seriously injured. He spits out blood and teeth, and in the hospital it turns out that he has brain hemorrhages, lung and liver injuries and he has lost all his sight. While he lies there in the chaos, he realizes that there is a terrorist attack in Norway.

In the government quarter where Føsker now works, eight people were killed and nine seriously injured. Norwegian terrorist Anders Behring Breivik killed 77 people, including many youths at a summer camp, before he was caught. In addition, he injured many for life, including Harald Føsker. For him personally, there have been many tough years in which he has had to learn to exercise, eat, walk, and to live as a visually impaired person. He currently has 20% vision.[2]

Føsker testified along with others who were directly affected in the trial of Anders Behring Breivik.

Even though he had his freedom cut dramatically, he is proud that we have a justice system and a correctional facility that treats everyone with respect and dignity.

"I haven't changed these attitudes and values," he said, face-to-face with the terrorist. Føsker has spent his entire professional life in the Norwegian Correctional Service. He is also the one who has trained the prison officers who will take care of the terrorist who, after the trial, receives a custodial sentence.

Føsker is proud that we have a legal system and a correctional facility that treats inmates with respect and dignity. This is based on the values all prison officers have learned in their education.

Our answer is more democracy, more openness, and more humanity. But never naivety.

- *Former Prime Minister Jens Stoltenberg's speech at Oslo Cathedral on July 24, 2011 (two days after the terror attack)*

In the days after the July 22 terror attacks, thousands of Norwegians across the country paraded with roses to commemorate those killed, support their relatives and distance themselves from terrorism. The TV images of Norwegians supporting each other in the crisis went around the world. "If one man can show so much hate, imagine how much love we can all show together," the young political social democrat Helle Gannestad wrote on Twitter. The quote was picked up by her political friend Stine Renate Håheim and was suddenly on everyone's lips. In response to the attack on Norwegian values, the Country's Prime Minister Jens Stoltenberg (now head of NATO) said this in response to the attack on Norwegian values: "Our answer is more democracy, more openness and more humanity. But never naivety."

But in the internal political circles, it boiled. The attack had also uncovered major deficiencies in emergency preparedness, and it was a particularly difficult time for the Minister of Justice Knut Storberget. The lawyer Storberget, who was now also the supreme political leader in the justice sector, was upset. He felt tremendous anger towards the mass murderer. At the same time, he had to face the criticism that Norway was not prepared for such a disaster. It was said about the incident that this was the worst attack in Norway since World War II. Norway is known as a small country without much crime, a country that has had politicians who, regardless of which parties they have belonged to, have invested in prevention, punishment that works and care for the victim. Norway is a country that has chosen a humane course in criminal law and a humane level of punishment where the police should not be armed. The prisons should ensure that those serving time are rehabilitated and able to avoid further offences.

Could this course continue after July 22, the event that affected everyone in Norway and even affected the outside world? Storberget reiterated Prime Minister Stoltenberg's desire for more openness and more democracy, but not naivety.

In a statement to the Parliament, Minister of Justice Knut Storberget pointed to seven challenges that needed to be addressed immediately. Among them was prevention of radicalization and extremism, methods used by the Norwegian Police Security Service (PST), response time, better communication and cooperation between police and defense, and to follow up with victims and next of kin.

The right way to react

Director Harald Føsker was in the hospital during the rose markings, and the days and weeks that followed, but is in retrospect happy that politicians reacted in the way they did. He has since worked with the Council of Europe and prepared a handbook on how to deal with radicalization and violent extremism for those in prison and custody.[3] But what happened in the correctional facility after the terror attack? Can they allow terrorists to have their civil rights as all inmates in Norway are entitled to? How will they follow up on the challenges outlined by the Attorney General?

More polarization in society and in correctional services

After the sudden terrorist attack that shocked the world, many eyes from abroad have been directed at Norwegian criminal care and the judiciary. The terrorist was sentenced to 21 years in custody, meaning he could theoretically be held in prison for life. He is still today serving his sentence in solitary confinement and has limited interactions with people. He is handcuffed as he leaves his cell to be taken to an air yard or work cell. He is also subjected to regular checks where he has to take off all his clothes. All communication in and out of the prison is controlled, and all contact in relation to visits and conversations with health personnel and lawyers is done through a glass wall. Otherwise, he has the same rights as everyone else. He has a normal cell at his disposal according to Norwegian conditions, and he also gets to study, even if he has to do that on his own. He must borrow books and receives little guidance.

PHOTO 12.1   Harald Føsker was on the 4th floor of the H-block in the Ministry of Justice when the bomb went off and destroyed the building on July 22, 2011. He was hospitalized for a long time

Source: Photo: Nina Hanssen

Prison as an area for radicalization

Prisons can be an arena for radicalization. Some inmates have vulnerability factors that can make them particularly vulnerable to different types of exposure.

As of April 2021, there were just over ten people charged, accused, or convicted of crimes related to terrorism or hate crimes in Norway.

Among them are inmates with right-wing extremist and extremist Islamist sympathies. The objective is that these should not be given the opportunity to form their own networks in prisons.[4] The Correctional Service's objective towards this group is, among other things, to prevent more people from being radicalized or grouped so that they constitute a power/threat factor to others and society.

The Norwegian Correctional Service has implemented some measures to prevent and deal with radicalization and violent extremism:

1. Radicalization coordinators in the regions
2. Radicalization contacts in the individual unit
3. Different educational programs for employees
4. Offer of mentoring measures to inmates.

It is challenging to ensure permanent integration into society for, among others, convicted terrorists. Here it is important that the employees have insight and understanding of the topic of radicalization and violent extremism. In Norwegian correctional services, a handbook has been prepared with the aim of giving officials working in prison increased knowledge on the topic of radicalization, adapting the overall plans to the work situation at the prison and clarifying expectations for handling.

The handbook treats radicalization and violent extremism as a phenomenon, while at the same time addressing more specifically the two main challenges we are confronted with in Norway: violent Islamism and right-wing extremism.

As early as 2018, guidelines were drawn for the Penal Execution Act, which deals with the prevention and management of radicalization and violent extremism in the Correctional Service. According to Naima Khawaja, who works with this field in the Norwegian Directorate of Correctional Services, the prevention of radicalization and violent extremism is an additional task that officials in the agency will work on. The objective for prisoners/convicts in this target group is the same as preventing new criminal offences.

The organization of the work aims to ensure that the necessary knowledge is given to employees so that they are better able to capture characters, features, and symbols.

Guidelines, structure and content

In 2014, the Ministry of Justice published an action plan against radicalization and extremism. Later, in 2018, guidelines for the Penal Execution Act were drawn up: "Prevention and management of radicalization and violent extremism in the Correctional Services." This was followed up by the government in 2020, which in its action plan also proposes, among other things, a mentoring scheme in the Correctional Services;[5] they will strengthen knowledge through education in the justice sector.

Purpose cannot work alone but needs coordination between the agencies. Municipalities have a way to go because of the strained economic situation.

What is a worldview team?

This is a team consisting of representatives from different faith and belief communities who, through work at the individual group and organizational level, will contribute to the prevention of radicalization. In addition, they will continue to focus on reducing present risk factors.

The mentoring scheme aims to motivate, support and create relationships with inmates and convicts in the hope of reducing the risk factors for channeling violent extremism.

Strengthen national coordination

The Directorate's group for follow-up and further development of the action plan against radicalization and violent extremism also focuses on cross-sectoral measures, says Naima Khawaja of the correction service.

Mentorship

She explains that the mentoring scheme in the Correctional Services is a targeted measure for the target group of prisoners/convicts who have been charged/convicted under the terrorism legislation provisions/hate speech, but also to inmates/convicts who may be vulnerable to exposure to being radicalized, during imprisonment.

The mentoring scheme was a three-year trial project that started in 2016. In a letter dated July 24, 2014, the Ministry of Justice and Public Security asked the Norwegian Directorate of Correctional Services to investigate the possibility of a mentoring scheme in the Correctional Services, as part of the government's other efforts to strengthen efforts to prevent radicalization and violent extremism. "A mentoring scheme will be developed and tested in the Correctional Services. The scheme will primarily target identified inmates who are understood to be vulnerable to being recruited for violent extremism, especially young inmates." The mentoring scheme was evaluated in February 2019.

A pilot with interfaith team

The work with an interfaith team is now a pilot project that will soon start in the east region of the correctional service in Norway.[6] Naima Khawaja of the Norwegian correctional authority says knowledge of signs and symbols forms the basis for officials sending messages of concern in accordance with guidelines. In addition, there is close cooperation between the Correctional Services, the police and especially PST on these cases.[1] Through interaction with these actors (between correctional services, the police and PST), information may also emerge that helps identify individuals in the target group, which forms the basis for concern and further follow-up.

With swastikas on the cell

One of the employees who has had to deal with tough cases as a prison officer when it comes to hatred of society is prison officer Farukh Qureshi in Oslo Prison.

Several times he has had to deal with radicalization in prison. He says that there are mostly two groups: those who misunderstand Islam, whom the authorities call Islamist terrorists; and those who fears the Jews and people of color, the so-called neo-Nazis. These groups have a growing hatred for society, a hatred that can develop into violent acts.

An example of this hatred can be found in the case where 15-year-old Benjamin Hermansen was stabbed to death at Holmlia in Oslo in January 2001. The boy had a Norwegian mother and Ghanaian father. That night, he was talking to a friend outside his convenience store when he was attacked by two young men belonging to a neo-Nazi group. The assault and murder were completely unprovoked and occurred only because of Benjamin's dark skin. The two young boys who committed the murder, Joe Erling Jahr and Ole Nicolai Kvisler, and a 17-year-old girl who took

---

1. The Norwegian Police Service is a national public service that will prevent crime and maintain safety for all citizens. The Norwegian Police Security Service (PST) is Norway's domestic security service, and is subordinate to the Ministry of Justice and Public Security. Its main task is to investigate and prevent serious offences that threaten national security.

part in it, received respectively 18, 17, and three years in prison. It is frightening to know that the neo-Nazi Ole Nicolai Kvisler, shortly after he was released from prison after serving 12 of 17 years for this murder, attended a Nazi camp. It turned out that Kvisler had had access to a worldwide Nazi community on the internet during his time in prison.[7] Qureshi wonders what, if anything, had been done to try to change his attitudes towards people of color. He is still pondering the question. What about the progression in the sentence, and why parole? The question he asked then was whether the correctional services – even after the terrorist incident on July 22 – look differently at Islamists and right-wing extremists, and the threat they pose to society.

Qureshi told *Aktuell*[8] *Magazine* that he had been set up as a contact officer for a Nazi who served time in Oslo Prison. The day before the inmate came up to the ward, he had drawn swastikas and hung them in his cell. Beforehand, Qureshi had read about the guy and his case and thought he shouldn't let this inmate make his workdays rotten. When the prison officer walked into his cell to introduce himself and greet him, he raised his hand, as he always does when meeting people, including inmates. Qureshi thought of a tip he had received from an inmate as an apprentice: "Always shake hands with inmates, listen to them, say 'No!' but hear what they have to say." There was no reaction from the man in front of him. Qureshi let his hand fall and said instead that he would like to have a conversation with him.

"I'm asleep," was the cold answer he received. The inmate turned his back to him in bed.

"Just ten minutes!" Qureshi said.

The man with the swastikas then reluctantly got up from the bed, and they entered the contact officer's room. It turned out that the inmate had no plans to talk in there either, and he didn't seem to listen to what Qureshi said. Then Qureshi took a piece of paper and wrote "0" and "10" on it. He then asked the inmate how much he hates the prison officer on a scale of zero to ten. A clear blush spread across the inmate's face, but he did not come up with an answer. Qureshi then asked the inmate to take a walk around the ward, and then come back again.

The inmate returned, and Quereshi gave him a new sheet on which he wrote "0" and "10."

"What about Mosa?" Qureshi asked. Mosa is another prison officer in the department. He's originally from Somalia. Still no answer from the inmate.

There were eventually many conversations with the man with the swastikas. Such conversations are important, Qureshi believes, and they must be put into place. It is demanding work, both human- and resource-wise. If they are to be able to do something about this problem, they need to strengthen dynamic security efforts, and that requires more staff, according to the prison officer. Qureshi wonders why neo-Nazi inmates feel that the prison does not see their group as a threat. Why do they get prison conditions where they have the opportunity to influence other inmates with their radical view of the world?

Qureshi thinks that if the prisoner had a non-Norwegian name and had similar hateful attitudes based on an Islamic view, he would probably have been perceived as a greater threat and ended up in Oslo Prison's most restrictive ward. In contrast to these, prisoners with a right-wing extremist background have been placed in the best wards at the prison. There should be no difference, he says. All types of extremism should be treated equally. The discrimination is visible and reinforces the feeling of exclusion and difference. Key words here are dynamic security work, seeing and listening to the prisoners, conversations and building trust, but that depends on whether there are enough employees.

Qureshi is happy to share several examples. A few years ago, they had in custody a terror-suspected inmate.

Qureshi eventually established a good relationship with him, something he already had with most others in this department. They had a lot of good conversations, and Qureshi tried to get the terror suspect to tell him what he was imprisoned for. He also tried to get the inmate to explain why he had committed the act that led to the indictment. It turned out that they had a very different view of how they understood the world, reality and the practice of religion. Over time, Qureshi observed that other inmates approached this inmate with questions about how to carry out prayer, and the

PHOTO 12.2 Prison officer Farukh Qureshi in Oslo Prison
Source: Photo by Nina Hanssen

terror suspect spent his time telling the other inmates that Muslims were the victims of injustice. Qureshi felt that he was trying to take on a role and spread a narrative that did not align with reality. Therefore, Qureshi tried to get an opportunity to address these topics in full, with other inmates present. On a weekend shift, he finally got an opportunity.

About half the ward was present in the common room that day, and they watched a football game. Then one of the inmates asked if Qureshi could print the prayer times for him. Qureshi used this as an approach to talk about different understandings of reality, different religious beliefs and practices, and different views of the world in general. Now he could talk to the terror suspect in front and at the same time with the other inmates. What he wanted with this conversation was to show the other inmates, using references to real events and by pointing to different perceptions of reality, that the narrative of the terror suspect was not correct. Qureshi challenged his view.

Good conversation

It was a good conversation, and afterwards several inmates pointed out that they appreciated that he addressed this topic for discussion. Most of the inmates respected him, therefore he could do this and in this way make the other inmates see that the narrative of the terror suspect was hollow and had more logical breaks than answers. The most interesting thing about this whole session was that the terror suspect felt that he lost his status and credibility among other inmates, but nevertheless he continued to both greet and discuss general social issues with Qureshi during his time in Oslo Prison.

Farukh Qureshi of Oslo Prison has five pieces of advice for colleagues to determine whether an inmate is radicalized:

1. Whatever the ideology, you see a change in inmates – take the conversation with employees
2. Seek cooperation with colleagues in workshops and school departments about the inmates' development.

3. Gain increased knowledge about the topic
4. Participate in a natural setting in the inmates' community and not just in the cell. It is important to be present and observant and interact in a natural setting.
5. Ensure that inmates have access to theologians regardless of religion.[9]

Notes

1. Personal communication 20.05.2022 with Harald Føsker, Oslo.
2. Personal communication with Harald Føsker.
3. Council of Europe handbook for prison and probation service redrawing radicalizing and violent extremism 16806f9aa9 (coe.int).
4. Personal communication with Naima Khawaja in the Directorate of Norwegian Correctional Service (KDI).
5. Action Plan against Radicalization and Violent Extremism (regjeringen.no).
6. Read more about interfaith team here: www.regjeringen.no/en/dokumenter/Action-plan-against-Radicalisation-and-Violent-Extremism/id762413/; https://krus.brage.unit.no/krus-xmlui/bitstream/handle/11250/2584996/Mentorordningen%20i%20kriminalomsorgen.pdf?sequence=1&isAllowed=y
7. Told to Mortensen, Yngvil, 2015 Frifagbevegelse.no.
8. Mortensen Yngvil, 2015 Gripping Farukh | Free Trade Movement.
9. Hanssen, N. (2019). Frifagbevegelse.no Radicalisation: Five signs prison staff must look for | FriFagbevegelse.no. Radikalisering: Fem tegn fengselsansatte må se etter | FriFagbevegelse.no.

13
THE CHALLENGE OF THE MENTALLY ILL AND THE USE OF ISOLATION IN PRISON – CRITICISM OF NORWEGIAN PRACTICE

> Dear prime minister. Violence and threats against employees in Norwegian prisons, isolation, and self-harm and suicide by inmates is worrying me. The highest risk of adverse events is in the first two weeks of custody. The most dangerous time is at nights.

Tommy Fredriksen represent the Norwegian Prison and Probation Officers, which is part of LO Norway. He continues his speech at the national Congress on June 1, 2022 in Oslo:

> What happens in prisons now is dangerous and I am worried about a de-politicization of the correction system. The pledge of rights cannot come at the expense of the security of inmates and employees. Staff is policy. Not only economy.

Fredriksen is challenging the Prime Minister Jonas Gahr Støre.
"Please do something about it. Now," he says, and the PM takes notes and walks up to the rostrum, promising to look into the problem.
The fact that many inmates have mental illnesses is obvious to people who work in the Correctional Services. The conditions for inmates with such disorders have been and remain a major concern for many employees. It's not always easy to know how to meet this group in prison. International and Norwegian reports show that the incidence of prisoners with mental illness is large and significantly higher than among the general population.

The statistics on the incidence of mental illness in prison are known through reports and assessments, but there is little scientific literature on how to deal with it.

A big challenge

The question of the mentally ill in prison intervenes in large and ethically difficult issues. Psychiatrist Randi Rosenqvist has for several years pointed out for that for[1] the inmates with major mental challenges, other and more appropriate measures are needed, because this group is most harmed by imprisonment. She has proposed some form of safety homes for them, and she believes such homes should be run by health trusts and not by municipalities or correctional services. The government has responded that it wants to try this out in a pilot project but is unsure who will be the best institution to run it.

DOI: 10.4324/9781003195887-13

Human mind

Our mental health affects how we think, feel, and act, and has a major impact on how we relate to others, experience stress or make choices. A person who has one or more diagnoses may have periods of physical, mental, and social well-being.

Randi Rosenqvist says there are hardly any inmates who have complete physical, mental, and social well-being, but adds that there are some inmates who are actually better off in prison than they are when they are out in society. Inmates who are rehabilitated, who have been given structure during the day and have an employment where they can relate to other people and experience mastery, will function better in prison than they do if they live on the street and are intoxicated.[2]

The research report from Fafo[3] in 2004 showed that a significant proportion have problems in relation to key areas of living such as education, income, housing, and health. "Many people have problems in several areas at the same time, and there is a clear correlation between the accumulation of living conditions problems and having been in prison multiple times."[4] In 2014, a new and more comprehensive survey was carried out with almost 900 convicted women and men, both Norwegian and foreign nationals, in 47 prisons. The survey, "Incidence of mental disorders in convicts in Norwegian prisons," was carried out by Victoria Cramer, who has researched psychiatric health conditions and disease prevalence both among inmates and in the general population. The survey found that among the convicts, as many as 92% at the time of the survey had signs of a personality disorder or mental illness. The survey also showed that the lifetime incidence of mental illness among prisoners is far higher than in the general population. Cramer stated that:[5]

- More than seven out of ten have at least one personality disorder
- More than six out of ten have both a personality disorder and one or more mental disorders
- More than four out of ten have an anxiety disorder
- More than two in ten have moderate/severe depression
- 2.5% have bipolar disorder
- Two out of ten have ADHD
- More than one in ten are at risk of suicide.

Complex challenges

In Cramer's survey, it was ascertained that the incidence of mental illness in prisons is significantly higher than in the rest of the population. Some are psychotic, others may be brain-damaged, mentally disabled or for other reasons not able to meet the "normal expectations" in prison care.

Randi Rosenqvist, who has been a forensic psychiatrist for many years, had her first patient in prison in 1978. She believes that the situation in Norwegian prisons has deteriorated as the number of beds in psychiatric health care has systematically been reduced.

Inmates are entitled to the same health services as the rest of the population, and at some prisons such as Ila, psychologists and psychiatrists are therefore employed.

Ila is different

Rosenqvist has for many years been employed as a senior adviser at Ila prison and detention center. This prison stands out in Norway because it is a detention facility for men. Detention was introduced into the Norwegian legal system in 2001. A person can be sentenced to custody if there is a high risk that he may repeat the crime or pose a danger to society. This can be said to be a sentence that is the same as life imprisonment in other countries. At Ila Detention and Security Prison, there have been many inmates struggling with long-term and complex challenges. Due to the inmates' situation, those at the prison have built up a cross-competence for the socially beneficial work of trying to help those who are struggling the most. Here they have motivated prison officers, program and environmental workers, sexologists, social workers, lawyers, and psychologists working across subjects to ensure good work with the inmates. When the detention scheme was adopted by the Storting, it was clear that the detainees should receive a better, rehabilitative punishment.

Rosenqvist believes that Cramer's survey still is important because it also maps the types of challenges in prison, but it does not say anything about those in custody. She believes there are even greater challenges there since most suicides are committed by inmates in custody. Custody is when a person is imprisoned while the offence for which he is suspected is being investigated. Among other things, the person concerned must be suspected of having committed an offence that will entail imprisonment for more than six months.

She believes the causes of suicide while in custody are that many people who are apprehended end up in some kind of shock and feel their lives collapse. Some also struggle with substance-abuse problems and simply undergo withdrawal. According to Seraf's living-conditions study, more than half of the inmates had used drugs daily in the six months before imprisonment. However, they are not free of the substance-abuse problems by the substance-abuse care taking control of their lives. The survey showed that 35% of the inmates used some form of medications or drugs to intoxicate themselves during previous or current prison stays.[6]

Suicide risk also over time

"It turns out that the longer a person has been in prison, the lower the risk of suicide, but the risk of suicide is still not quite over," she says.

One who has done a lot of research on suicide in Norwegian correctional services is prison and suicide researcher Dr. Philos Yngve Hammerlin. His first report on 49 suicides in the period 1956–1987 received great international attention when this was[7] a relatively unknown problem at the time, and it was an area of little research. In a sub-report that came shortly afterwards, he interviewed inmates who had been close to committing suicide. The report was highly critical of the detention institute, the use of isolation and inadequate follow-up from psychiatry in the prison service. Hammelin's critical voice and analytical and scientific approach to Norwegian correctional services have been listened to, and in particular, KROM and the trade unions for prison employees in Norway have taken in more of his thoughts. Detention today remains critical for many inmates. In the late 1980s, politicians began debating whether they should establish a "gray-area facility," a special prison for convicts with major behavioral deviations. In 1992, a proposal to the Storting[8] was made to establish such a special prison inspired by the Dutch TBS institutions (Interdisciplinary Specialized Treatment of Substance-Abuse Disorders).[9]

Other measures adopted were a two-year trial project at Ila Prison. This was supposed to be a response to criticism of the extremely difficult prison conditions for those who were struggling with mental-health challenges.

In his latest book, Hammerlin calls for more cooperation between prison and professional staff, such as teachers and librarians who are not subject to the Correctional Services, but still have their work in prison (so-called imported services). "Cooperation with some agencies in some contexts can sometimes be a bit difficult, and problems with cooperating with NAV are mentioned in connection with certain prisons. Today as before prisons are also struggling to transfer suicidal and severely mentally suffering prisoners to psychiatric institutions for treatment," he said.[10]

In guidelines for the prevention and management of self-harm, suicide attempts and suicide in prison, the list of risk factors for suicide in prisoners was also expanded to apply to crises and relationship problems, negative future prospects, social isolation and low impulse control.[11]

Too few beds

Figures from Statistics Norway (SSB) show that one of three psychiatric beds in the health service have disappeared since 1990.[12] Randi Rosenqvist assumes that this is mostly due to economics but she has also noticed that there has been an anti-psychiatry wave in Europe and in the United States. At the same time, the Correctional Services in Norway have experienced large cuts in the economy for several years and therefore have somewhat less resources to assist the very sickest. It must be noted that even with eight years of cuts to this offer, Norway is still one of the countries that spends the most resources on helping prisoners with mental-health problems.

Respect and clear communication

For Rosenqvist, the most important thing is that the inmates are met with respect and clear communication. Employees must also be careful to report so that deviant behavior is recorded. And prison officers need to communicate to understand if there is reason to send a message of concern to the health service. She says that this information from the Correctional Services will be an important premise in doctors' assessments of admission. Even if an inmate is discharged from a psychiatric institution, there is no evidence that he is fully recovered. And if he or she is rapidly deteriorating again, the Correctional Services should consider whether he or she is able to serve their sentence or should be given a break in the penance, if it is justifiable in terms of safety.

PHOTO 13.1 Former governor Knut Bjarkeid in front of Ila Prison
Source: Photo: Jan-Erik Østlie

At Ila Detention and Security Prison, they have had convicts in custody with serious sufferings for years. This was also why they established the resource team which Rosenqvist was a part of.

Rosenqvist has the following recommendations for prison employees who are in contact with inmates who are struggling mentally:[13]

1. "Show the prisoner the same respect in conversations that you would show your mother or boyfriend.
2. It is right to be direct when it comes to critical comments, but it may then be appropriate also to say something positive
3. Keep in mind that many inmates have experienced a long row of rejections and disappointments and that they often reject the one they talk to with the purpose of avoiding the pain of being rejected again.
4. Some inmates need a very long time to become familiar with a person. Don't expect an inmate to treat everyone equally. Respect colleagues who have built up a good relationship with an inmate, but if you find that only you understand an inmate, you may want to ask for some guidance. The staff shall treat the inmate equally, and one should be loyal to what has been decided.
5. Always keep your promises, never make any that you can't keep. Avoid using terms like 'might,' 'we'll see,' 'it's possible,' and so on, if you don't at the same time explain what it depends on.
6. Speak in short and full sentences if possible. Be aware that many people have difficulty following longer reasoning, and they do not speak up if they do not understand what is being said. People who are in a mentally unstable situation will experience this more sharply. Sometimes it may be appropriate to ask them to repeat what you said.
7. If you get annoyed or impatient in the conversation, try to mute your nonverbal reaction and say clearly: 'When you do this, I get annoyed, and then it is difficult for us to cooperate and talk. Can you be so kind as to answer what I'm asking?'
8. If you've done or said something stupid, bring it up with the inmate and apologize."[14]

Prison in prison

By being placed in solitary confinement in prison, even stricter restrictions are imposed on inmates. This may include reduced or minimal contact with other inmates and staff, exclusion from joint activities and restrictions on visits. The European Court of Human Rights (ECHR) has described isolation as an "Imprisonment within the prison."[15]

Isolation is the most invasive means of power for the inmates, and the practice evokes issues of due process, Norway's international obligations and our own self-image as a nation. It is well documented that isolation is very stressful and entails a high health risk for the person being isolated. Practice and research show that we negatively react physically, mentally and emotionally to isolation, and there is broad agreement that this is harmful.

The main rule in Section 17 of the Penal Code is that all prisoners in Norwegian prisons shall, as far as practicable, have access to others during work, training, program activities and in their spare time. This basically means that they should have access to community and social contact with other inmates throughout the day, from morning to evening. Today, the Norwegian Correctional Services are aware of the negative consequences of isolation, but there are still major challenges in Norwegian correctional services. The Scandinavian isolation network was launched at the annual conference of the Norwegian Association for[16] Criminal Justice Reform (KROM) in 2014. This conference marked a new form of public conversation about isolation. Among the presenters there were people who had been isolated themselves, in addition to relatives, psychologists and lawyers from different Nordic countries. The other participants were prison leaders, officers, doctors, researchers, lawyers and experts from the UN and the Council of Europe in addition to the torture-monitoring committee from the Council of Europe and the UN, as well as the Parliamentary Ombudsman, Norwegian defense lawyers and Swedish prosecutors.

The Penal Execution Act of May 18, 2001 no. 21, is based on a community principle where the main rule pursuant to Article 17 is that prisoners shall have a community with other prisoners.[17]

Nevertheless, isolation, "exclusion from the community" and "use of coercive measures" are still considered necessary instruments, in order to ensure safe and sound punishment.

Criticism of Norway's use of isolation and custody

The Norwegian Correctional Service has received criticism from both national and international monitoring bodies for the use of exclusion and isolation in Norwegian prisons. The mentioned criticism has been made by, among others, the Parliamentary Ombudsman, the Norwegian National Institution for Human Rights (NIM), the Council of Europe's Torture-Monitoring Committee (CPT), UN Torture Committee (CCPR) and Council of Europe Torture Committee (CAT).

Isolation in prisons is a challenge that is difficult to solve. An example is shown in the case of mass murderer Anders Behring Breivik taken to the Norwegian legal system and the European Court of Human Rights in Strasbourg. He believed that the degree of isolation directed at him by the state was contrary to human rights. Breivik complained that Norway violated Article 3 of the European Convention on Human Rights (inhuman and degrading treatment) and Article 8 (the right to privacy), related to his prison conditions. The terrorist has been locked up, mostly in complete isolation, since July 22, 2011, after bombing the government quarter and committing mass shootings on Utøya. Breivik then had a cell with three rooms, and an apparatus by staff to socialize him, including a paid "visiting friend."[18] This was not good enough for Breivik, who believed that he should have more contact with ordinary inmates. The prison management felt this was not possible and referred to Breivik's own security. In the Court of Appeals' decision, it is pointed out, among other things, that there is an ongoing risk of violence both from and against Breivik.[19]

In June 2017, the European court of human rights (EcHR) in Strasbourg dismissed Breivik's appeal because they did not find that his human rights had been violated.[20]

Norway, however, has listened to criticism from EcHR in other cases, and the response from Norway has been the formation of a national community department for long-term isolation at Ila Detention and Security Prison, as well as 11 activity and resource teams to ensure that those who are isolated for various reasons remain active and have a possibility to come out of the cell.

How we make a slightly better everyday life in prison

In 2023, a new building will open at Ila Prison, with room for six inmates. Gaby Groff-Jensen, first prison officer/coordinator for the National Community Division (NFFA), is pleased.

The unique department's task is to provide meaningful companionship and activities to male inmates who have been excluded from the recreational community for a long time (long-term isolation) due to acting out or conspicuous behaviors caused by serious and complex problems, and where it cannot be ruled out that it is due to severe mental illness. Groff-Jensen says that NFFA was established in a temporary department at Ila Prison on January 1, 2020 and has now been moved to the Romerike prison department at Ullersmo, during the ongoing rehabilitation of the buildings at Ila.

Interdisciplinary team

The staffing in the department is funded by both the Ministry of Health and Care Services and the Ministry of Justice and Public Security, and will have employees with both health and prison expertise. The target groups here are those who have long been isolated due to problematic behaviors in prison such as violent behavior, who pose a risk to both inmates and staff, those who are in the gray area between prison and psychiatry, and mentally ill inmates.

"Our goal is to create a better quality of life for the long-term isolated and get them out of isolation," says Groff Jensen. This can best be done through active and interpersonal contact and good environmental work. "We think outside the box, across common routines and guidelines and try to give the vulnerable as good a prison sentence as possible. When they least deserve it, they get it anyway," she says, since they focus not only on the behavior but the reason behind it. By reducing the use of isolation, they hope to achieve the goals of being able to create a better quality of life for long-term isolated people and minimize isolation damage.

Communication is important

Gaby Groff-Jensen says that they focus on interaction and communication to create a safe and predictable relationship. For the team, it is to show good attitudes and respect, it is not a struggle to show who's in charge. She says,

> We want to give inmates choices and co-determination through responsibility for their own lives because we believe responsibility provides coping and motivation. We must never underestimate inmates, even when we think they make bad choices for themselves. Maybe that's all they're capable of. We must be the professional part that positively motivates and facilitates inmates to make good choices for themselves.

Facts about the resource team at Ila

In 2014, the Parliament allocated money to a resource team at Ila Detention and Security Prison. The team became interdisciplinary, and they started work on motivating the long-term isolated inmates with mental disorders with the aim of counteracting the negative harmful effects of isolation with the vision of "a slightly better day." Despite the good results the resource team has achieved over five years of operation, challenges have been associated with both localities and expertise. The need for modern and adapted premises pushed forward, while at the same time cooperation with psychiatric wards and their competence constantly evolved. In the national budget for 2019, funding was therefore allocated for the establishment of a separate prison ward with up to six places for this group of inmates. Funding was allocated over the budgets of both the Ministry of Health and the Ministry of Justice to staff the department, so that it would consist of employees with both prison and health expertise.

Notes

1. Randi Rosenqvist is originally American, but grew up in Trondheim and Oslo. She is today the most high-profile Norwegian forensic psychiatrist who works in the Norwegian Correctional Services. She has previously worked as a consultant physician at Aker Hospital.
2. Rosenqvist, R. (2019). Care and follow-up of prisoners with mental disorders page 206, knowledge-based penal execution in Norway. These quotes are from personal communication with Randi Rosenqvist in her home in Oslo, May 2022.
3. Fafo is an independent social science research foundation in Norway that develops knowledge on the conditions for participation in working life, organisational life, society and politics, the relationship between politics and living conditions, as well as on democracy, development and value creation. https://fafo.no
4. Friestad, C., & Hansen, S. (2004). *Living conditions among prisoners*. Oslo: Fafo.
5. Ibid.
6. Health and substance abuse challenges in prisons ACTIS NOTE 1:2020 The experiences of employees. Actis Note 1: 2020.

7. Hammerlin, Y., & Bødal, K. (1988). Suicide in Norwegian prisons from 1956–1987. Oslo, Norway: Oslo Ministry of Justice (Correctional Services).
8. White Paper 56–1991–1992.
9. Interdisciplinary specialised treatment of substance abuse disorders (TSB) is the term for the treatment of substance abuse and addiction treatment at a specialist level.
10. Hammerlin, Y. (2021). Hard mot de harde, myk mot de myke - norsk kriminalomsorg i anstalt. Uniiversitetsforlaget.
11. Kriminalomsorgsdirektoratet, 2018.
12. SSB selvmordsstatistikk.
13. Rosenqvist, R., Chapter 10 page 222.
14. Rosenquvist, R. (2018). Chapter: ivaretakelse og oppfølging av innsatte med psykiske lidelser page 206 in the book «kunnskapsbasert straffegjennomføring i kriminalomsorgen i Norge.»
15. Piechowicz vs. Poland (2012) section 165.
16. www.isolation.network.
17. OT.prp.nr 4 (2000–2001) side 70.
18. www.nrk.no/norge/_-besoksvennen-en-profesjonell-aktor-1.13327484)
19. www.nrk.no/norge/breiviks-klage-pa-soningsforholdene-avvist-av-strasbourg_-_-dette-lopet-er-sluttfort-1.14093635
20. www.dagbladet.no/nyheter/anders-behring-breivik-fikk-avvist-klagesaken-mot-norge/69922932

14
WOMEN IN NORWEGIAN PRISONS

International correctional research says that there is a tendency for women to have more stringent security procedures than necessary when they have committed a criminal act. But what are the conditions like for women in Norwegian prisons today?

Approximately 5% of prisoners in Norway today are women. As of February 2022, there is a total of 184 women serving sentences, 180 of which are serving in prison. 59 of these are serving custody, 9 are serving a custodial sentence, 5 are serving sentences in transitional housing and 49 are in low security.[1]

There are four prisons for women in Norway: Bredtveit, Ravneberget, Kragerø and Evje. In addition, in some prisons with a high level of security, there are also specially adapted women's wards. These can be found in Trondheim, Bergen and Kongsvinger.

Bredtveit Prison in Oslo is the only detention center for women in Norway. Here the average sentence is seven years, but in the other prisons where women are serving, the sentence is lower.

In Norway, there are 27 women serving sentences for murder, 11 for bodily injury, ten for violence against a public official and 42 for drug-related crimes. There are three women serving sentences for rape and four for morality crimes.

Bredtveit Prison was originally built as a home for boys long before the Second World War and was used as a prison for female traitors after the war.

According to researcher Yngve Hammerlin,[2] interest in the situation of female inmates increased in the 1970s after Kåre Bødal wrote an appendix called "women in prison" to the report on the prison system. This was based on a study he made of women in Bredtveit Prison in 1972. The study aroused interest and the Ministry began to take a closer look at prison conditions for women. Until then, they had very little information on the needs and situation of female prisoners. After Bødal's report, the Ministry began to make a systematic view of the situation for female prisoners and the future need for places for women. Then criticism of poor prison conditions for women began to come from various sources.

A separate committee on female prisoners

Researcher Hammerlin was invited in 1987 to sit on a Women's Reconciliation Committee chaired by District Court Judge Ingrid E. Solheim, who herself had a strong humanistic view of man. The committee was to look further at women's prison conditions. The unique thing about this work was that a former inmate also participated in securing the prisoner perspective. A two-part report

DOI: 10.4324/9781003195887-14

from the committee was presented to the minister in 1989. It addressed women's prison conditions, including the situation of female inmates with children. In the mandate they had, they should look at mother/child imprisonment. "In 1989, an average of 77 women were imprisoned in Norwegian prisons at any given time. This accounted for around 4 per cent of inmates in Norwegian prisons. Of these, 41 were sentences, 29 were in custody, three were in closed prisons and four were imprisoned for fines."[3] They expected the number of female inmates to increase.

The management at Bredtveit Prison followed up in the 1990s with measures on the best of their ability from the resources they had at their disposal. At the time director Dan Strømme took an important position in the new parent/child committee in the 1990s, and the committee was supported by several. The pressure to improve prison conditions for women meant that they got a slightly better schooling offer and better open-prison conditions, but there were still challenges. In the 1990s, the Equality Ombudsman followed up the Women's Atoning Committee's recommendations and their proposals, but was not satisfied with the progress. A new committee was appointed in 1994 to follow up the sub-report on mothers with children as reflected in White Paper 27 1997/1998 on the Penal Execution Act. After a working group wrote the report "Equal prison conditions between women and men" written by Hilde Lundeby, KDI adopted strategy for women in custody and penal execution 2017–2020.[4] The purpose of the strategy was for women to be ensured equal terms as men. Nevertheless, criticism continued from the Parliamentary Ombudsman, the Equality Ombudsman and Legal Advice for Women (JURK[5]). Female inmates still face distinctive challenges. Because there are so few prison places for women, it is challenging for convicted women to be allowed to serve time in their local communities where they have their families and network.

In White Paper 39, we find this quote: "The principle of proximity entails that the convicts shall, as far as possible, carry out the punishment near the place of residence." Furthermore:

> Since there are few female inmates, it will always be more difficult to uphold both the principle of carrying out punishments near their place of residence (the principle of proximity) and the principle that women and men should be separated in their own prisons or wards. The Correctional Services must balance the principle of proximity and the police's needs during the custody period on the one hand and a content of the penal execution specially adapted for women on the other.[6]

Because women and children numerically constitute small groups of inmates, they shall in principle be shielded from male and adult inmates respectively and also have an offer that is equivalent to the provision to other inmates. But the report emphasizes that it can be difficult to combine with the principle of proximity, with exceptions not discussed further, only that it must be "weighed against other important considerations, including the need for competence and safety."

The Gender Equality and Distribution Ombudsman[7] in Norway has pointed this out several times. The Ombudsman has said that isolation of women and other discrimination between women and men is often explained by the fact that the women are in a minority and that differential treatments thus affect fewer inmates. Other things the Ombudsman has pointed out are that the buildings are older in typical women's prisons such as in Bredtveit and Kragerø. Nor has the offer of school or work been of the same quality and quantity for female inmates compared to the offer to male inmates.

A survey on women's prison conditions was carried out between August 2019 and May 2020 by the Department of Criminology and Sociology of Law (University of Oslo) based on 36 informants.

The report, which was published as «Lengst inne i fengselet - kvinnelige innsatte med behov for helsehjelp» "at the far end of the[8] prison-female inmates in need of health care". Translated as "Deep inside the prison – female inmates in need of health care" published by the University i Oslo from the perioden 2020 to 2021, tells us about isolation, struggling conditions and widespread self-harm among female inmates in Norwegian prisons.

PHOTO 14.1   Former prisoner "Luna Vanatta" in Bredtveit Prison became an artist in prison

Source: Photo: Nina Hanssen

Staff reported that female inmates still have a higher incidence of both mental and physical health problems than men do. There is an accumulation of living-condition problems among female inmates, and many are severely traumatized as a result of both sexual assault and prostitution, and often have more substance-abuse challenges than men but lack treatment options. Many people struggle with anxiety and severe depression, and they often also have suicidal thoughts both before and during their sentences. The report says the mentally ill are placed in smooth cells but become like balls bounced between prison and psychiatry in the absence of adequate help.

The women themselves tell of widespread self-harm and violent reactions, and the employees say they lack professional assistance and programs to assist the women, and there is also a shortage of female doctors.

Norwegian prison saved me

One of those who has served many years in Norwegian prisons far away from family is Russian Luna Vanatta. She initially served time in Stavanger, but was later transferred to Kongsvinger Prison, which established a separate department for foreign women with deportation decisions. It was in Kongsvinger Prison that Vanatta was introduced to an art teacher who made her paint. Suddenly Vanatta, who had struggled with a lot of anxiety and depression, found a way to express herself, and in the last six months she served in Bredtveit Prison, she painted a lot. Just a few weeks before she was released, she had a large art exhibition in Grorud Church not far from the prison.

Clearly affected by the intense situation between Ukraine and Russia, the artist behind the walls also painted several paintings about the unrest she felt inside. The rest of her exhibition is about different aspects of women's lives.

Vanatta says that she has expressed light, shadow, violence, values, grief, care and, not least, joy. The rest are acrylic images, including one that resembles a more modern version of *Mona Lisa*.

She doesn't know how she has managed to paint so beautifully, but thinks it just turned out that way. Vanatta has never painted before and had no idea that this was something she could do, but her teacher had faith in her. "That was the kick I needed to start my new life," she says proudly. The inspiration for the exhibition, which she has called *Femina*, comes from experiences she has had both before and during her sentence in Norwegian prisons.

She tells us of a dark time in which it felt like she had reached rock bottom, where she also planned to take her own life and made the worst choice of her life. Now she feels stronger than ever. During her stay in prison, she managed to find herself again. Now she wants to use art to reach out to others who feel alone and helpless.

The dream is that her paintings can help someone else to choose the right path without hurting themselves or others. Vanatta has served four years in Norwegian prison and has spent much of the time alone in her cell. That was what made her first meeting with the prison and the other inmates so impactful. She was depressed and very affected by the big difference between her and the other inmates. Their values and mentality clashed with hers. Through her artwork, she had her head cleaned, and she describes it as a revelation. Some of the images show both violence and gloomy thoughts.

She thinks it almost sounds a bit strange, but sometimes she thinks that those women who are victims of physical violence are a little lucky because it appears on the outside. Anyone can see it with the naked eye. "If you have been a victim of psychological violence, it is difficult to see," she says.

Vanatta found her strengths and values during her sentence. Now she knows exactly what she wants to do in the future, and hopes she can continue with her art. It makes her happy and lighter at heart.

Governor Doris Bakken at Bredtveit Prison participates in Vanatta's exhibition and feels proud and happy. The Norwegian Correctional Service has once again succeeded in making an inmate feel mastery and joy. She wishes Vanatta the best of luck as it is only a matter of days before she is out. We follow Bakken back to her office to see how things are going in the country's largest women's prison.

PHOTO 14.2 Governor Doris Bakken at Bredtveit Prison is the head of the largest women's prison in Norway.

Source: Photo: Nina Hanssen

Female prison director

Doris Bakken is passionate about women's prison conditions and enjoys her job here. She has previously worked in Ila Detention and Security Prison, Oslo Prison and in the Romerike prison department at Ullersmo prison before becoming head of the largest women's prison in Norway. According to KRUS, the distribution between female and male officers in Norway is now around 50/50, but there are the most female employees in purely female prisons.

She says,

> It is an advantage that we have the most female employees considering that it is then slightly better for the inmates in terms of safety, control measures such as saliva samples and other measures. In addition, it is easier for the inmates to discuss typical women's issues with female officers.

Bakken is pleased that Norway has had a good development with several female employees in the Correctional Services since the 1980s.

> There are closed security and control routines in prisons and now we have recently received a new revised strict rule when it comes to body searches. But what is particularly positive for female inmates is that we will now go from urine sample to saliva sample and use body scanners to a greater extent.

The Norwegian Directorate of Correctional Services (KDI) has recently ordered prisons to end the practice of routine body searches and random sampling, following a ruling in Gulating Court of Appeal[9] in 2020.

She says,

> For women who have experienced abuse, these checks can almost be perceived as a new abuse and many feel violated when they must undress and pee while others are watching. It is much better for women to stand with normal clothes and take saliva samples with swabs.

Many struggles with mental health

Doris Bakken is also concerned with the frustration many employees feel towards all the inmates who have mental illnesses. International and Norwegian reports show that the incidence of prisoners with mental illnesses is large and significantly higher than among the general population.

Particularly vulnerable group

Doris Bakken at Bredtveit Prison says that there are many inmates with mental-health challenges here too.

She sadly says,

> Some of those in prison are slightly mentally disabled. Some are very outspoken, and I sometimes wonder if they are able to be imprisoned. We tend to have around three to four people coming in from reinforced housing and some are mentally at the eight- to 15-year stage. Some of them remain in custody for a long time, and some receive mental-health care, but unfortunately some also stay in a security cell because they do everything they can to commit suicide.

"There is a lot of suffering among them, and this is a tiny group in society that falls outside. They are the crossing point between psychiatry, prison and the police," she says, referring to some of the media cases in which mentally ill people or "lonely wolves" have committed crimes with major consequences, such as the 2021 killings. A 38-year-old man went berserk with various weapons, killed five civilians and injured several in a street in the small Norwegian town of Kongsberg in October 2021.

She says,

> These people are expensive for society and dangerous for other people. That's why I think it is unfair they're not taken care of so they could be saved from doing so much harm because they're not being treated for their illness.

She thinks it is thought-provoking that we as a rich welfare society fail in preventing the development of crime among this vulnerable group.

"We are dealing with people who are initially vulnerable and who may also find themselves in a vulnerable life situation," she says. Doris Bakken is pleased that the new government has granted extra resources to resource teams at Bredtveit Prison working with the mentally ill group. The detention team has also had a few extra resources. It's the right move as there are so many inmates struggling and a staff who are frustrated because they don't know how to meet this group.

"There's a contradiction in the fact that we're going to do correctional services. We are part of society's power apparatus at the same time as the prisons are a place where care, rehabilitation, development and change will also take place," she says, and admits that it has been extra demanding to achieve this during the pandemic.

She says,

> The punishment is detention and we have worked a lot to make sure that the inmates receive a good offer. The requirement is at least two hours of quality time together with other people, but we will strive for at least eight hours, preferably 12. We can do this on weekdays, but due to a shortage of staff, we can't manage more than six to seven hours on weekends, but we are probably higher than the average in other prisons.

Bakken believes that those with mental-health challenges often can end up in a vicious cycle where they are incarcerated and become more isolated. This will exacerbate their ailments.

She says,

> When people are removed from society and at the same time isolated in a prison cell away from their loved ones, this can feel extremely heavy. The number of female inmates with children is high, and many inmates are still far away from family and networks. There are few suicides among female inmates, but we have many suicidal women and many who engage in life-threatening self-harm. We have managed to save the lives of many women over the years, and we are glad we have a good cooperation with many organizations and the public sector, when the inmates are released. Because, as we've heard before, Norwegian prisons are run according to the so-called import model. In practice, this means that various agencies in the community provide services to inmates in prisons, in the same way that they also provide these services outside prison. Examples of such services are health services, school/education, NAV services and library services. All inmates have access to guidance and assistance from the state Labor and Welfare Administration and the parts of the municipalities' social services that are included in the joint local offices also called NAV.

NAV's work in Bredtveit Prison

The focus of NAV's work is employment in the last part of the sentence and in the period after release. The cooperation between NAV and the Norwegian Correctional Services is regulated in agreements at national and local levels. The Correctional Services are run according to the so-called import model, i.e., different agencies in society provide services to inmates in prisons, in the same way that they also provide these services to people outside prisons.

NAV is one of these agencies in the same way that school, health, crisis centers and Stifinner'n are. Stifinner'n is an offer to inmates with substance-abuse and addiction problems.

The women at Bredtveit can contact NAV directly or via call tags, but it can also be done by employees in the Norwegian Correctional Services or other services who see a need.

NAV's work in the various prisons is adapted to local conditions, i.e., the inmate group, location, and resources available in the prison. At Bredtveit Prison, a supervisor from NAV is employed in a full-time position. NAV assists inmates with contact to their local NAV office during their sentence. The main focus is work/employment/treatment and income protection upon release. One way NAV helps to stay focused on post-release work is to qualify the women during their sentences. NAV has been organizing courses at Bredtveit Prison since 2000. It was the first prison in Norway to try this and it became so successful that several prisons followed suit. The courses are adapted to the labor market and the portfolio is dynamic. They have held courses on construction gardeners, lifts, trucks, flower bindings and baristas. Dog courses have also been carried out.

"The courses are very popular among the inmates. In addition to giving competence, it gives the participants hope and new mastery. This can act like a counterweight to the injuries resulting from long sentences," says NAV consultant Tone Bremnes, who works with the women at Bredtveit.

Notes

1. Kriminalomsorgen.no.
2. Hammelin, Y. (2021). Hard against the hard, soft against the soft (universitetsforlaget.no) page 188. Oslo, Norway.
3. Figures from the Summary on women's prison conditions, Ministry of Justice/Criminal Division, 1089, Chapter 5.
4. Strategy+for+women+in+custody+and+penal execution.pdf
5. Legal advice for women (**JURK**) are female law students who offer free, customized self-help assistance for anyone who defines themselves as women.
6. White Paper 39 page 9 Notify. St. 39 (2020–2021) (regjeringen.no).
7. The Equality and Anti-Discrimination Ombud handles the legislation in relation to prohibitions against discrimination. This combines to the four anti-discrimination laws (the Equality Act, the Anti-Discrimination Act on Ethnicity, the Anti-Discrimination Act on Sexual Orientation and The Anti-Discrimination and Accessible Rights) together into the Equality and Prohibition of Discrimination Act.
8. Marion Hellebust, Peter Scharff Smith, Ingrid Lundeberg and May-Len Skilbrei, (2021) Department of Criminology and Sociology of Law Gluing/Plastic Folder-A4> (ldo.no).
9. Response Letter-from-KDI.pdf (sivilombudsmannen.no).

15
TROND LEAVES THE PRISON FOR THE LAST TIME

The prisoner in Halden Prison Trond Henriksen looks at the watch. The sun is shining. He has been a heavy drug addict, bank robber, kidnapper, and thief, in addition a period when he was described as "Norway´s most dangerous prisoner." Today he packs down his clothes and personal belongings. It is only minutes until he shall walk out of the transitional housing which is placed close to the walls of Halden Prison, with the same thoughts every released person has: This is absolutely the last time. After a long and tough struggle through many years, with many ups and downs, he is finally drug-free and on his way to freedom.

Payback time

Not all released people are as lucky as Trond, with such a smooth transition to society after imprisonment. It doesn't work out for many of them. Too many! Through hard work and motivation,

PHOTO 15.1 Prisoner Trond Henriksen interviews governor Are Høidal for Radio Prime, a local radio station in Halden

Source: Photo: Halden prison

DOI: 10.4324/9781003195887-15

Trond has managed to get himself a place to live and a job in the city of Halden. He settles down here. Now he has a job in the radio, and he loves it. You see, he is host in a robber radio that is sent out on the FM network, on Radio Prime. This is his entrance ticket to the ordinary working life.

Soon he will meet his love too. They decide to live together. He is so grateful, but his conscience can't let him rest. Trond knows he has cost the Norwegian society about 150 million Norwegian kroner. How can he pay this back to the society? He writes a book and gives special thanks to his mom. He feels badly about everything he's put her through. In 2015 Trond is offered a job in Church City Mission. Here he runs a café, makes movies, and starts many projects. He is engaged in getting youths to stay in school until they are finished and talks freely about his experiences behind bars. Trond is convinced that he has succeeded because he has met prison officers who have seen him and heard him. Nothing in life is more important than that. The tight and close relationships, with those he calls the pearl people, has meant everything to him. And another role model who has been important is a man who was imprisoned at approximately the same time as him: Nelson

PHOTO 15.2 Governor Are Høidal in Halden Prison was proud to work in the Norwegian prison service known for being heavily focused on rehabilitation

Source: Photo: Halden Prison

74 Trond leaves the prison for the last time

Mandela. Trond was fascinated and inspired by Mandela's words and the power of love that he found in them, and he wrote sayings from Mandela on the wall of his cell. Even after he was released, he has thought a lot on how Mandela managed the transition from imprisonment back into society. Despite extremely tough years in prison, he managed to see what was positive in both people and situations and talked about reconciliation, reconciliation, reconciliation. This has inspired Trond, who now is the leader of a project called "young at daytime" that is meant to help youths with problems. Trond knows a lot about those problems. The circle is complete. It feels meaningful. It is extremely good to know that he can help youths to choose another way than he chose. At least he can try to help. He knows it is not easy. He has tried many times. That makes him know what he talks about. His dream is to give something back and use his life to prevent, and avoid, others ending up in the same hopeless situation he once was in. Soon the building he has dreamt about for so long will be finished. He himself has managed to get 25 million Norwegian kroner as financial support to what they call "Byparken." The governor Are Høidal looks Trond Henriksen in his eyes as a free man and gives him a solid handshake and a hug.

"You can make it. I believe in you," the governor says.

"Thank you dad," the former prisoner replies.

16
RELEASE TO FREEDOM – MIND THE GAP

The wind howls and huge waves break against the boat as it struggles in the storm on the open sea. It is cold and the saltwater splashes in his face, but the former UN soldier and prison officer Stian Estenstad feels warm and satisfied when he observes how employees and inmates from the prison cooperate to maneuver the boat. Soon they will get sight of the coast of Trøndelag on the horizon, and he is looking forward to telling his boss, Thorvald Stoltenberg, about another successful boat trip directed by the Red Cross.

Viking blood

Stian Estenstad says,

> There is something very old and genuinely Norwegian with these boat trips made exactly like those from the Viking period. We have arranged these trips every year since 2006 and with about 50 persons on board we are sailing along the coast of Norway in all kinds of weather. This trip creates unity, and we are getting shared experiences and relations that last.

> He is the driving force behind these unique boat trips which are arranged by the Red Cross in partnership with Norwegian prison care. He says that when they are on board these boats, the past and the future almost disappear, and everyone is together and present in the moment. This is therapeutic for both inmates and officers, he thinks. Estenstad has worked in Oslo Prison for many years, and before that he worked as a driver and lifeguard for former Foreign Minister Johan Jørgen Holst. He has also worked as a driver for the famous reporter Robert Fisk in the Middle East when he was an FN soldier. Estenstad has always been concerned with people, and when he worked for the TOG project (Measures Against Repeat Offenders) for three years he had seen an enormous gap between the great job they did in Norwegian prison care and the needs the former inmates have when they were released. They have more problems than the average population in areas such as upbringing, physical and mental health, alcohol and drugs, work, education, housing, economy and relationships with family and friends.

He says,

> I have heard people say that they felt more secure in the prison cell than in their own home and that a new punishment started the day they were released. Being referred to as a client,

DOI: 10.4324/9781003195887-16

PHOTO 16.1 Stian Estenstad in the Red Cross organizes unique boat trips for prisoners and former prisoners

Source: Photo: Red Cross

user, patient, inmate, drug addict, or resident can do something with our mind. Some feel marginalized, incapacitated, passivated and clientified when they leave prison.

More than visiting service

As almost everywhere else in the world, volunteers in the Red Cross aid people who need help and support. Among other things, they have a visiting service where volunteers visit inmates in

PHOTO 16.2 On board these Viking boats the past and the future almost disappear, as both inmates and officers are together and present in the moment

Source: Photo: Red Cross

Norwegian prisons and in addition to that, the Red Cross in Norway is engaged in helping former prisoners. It was the former president in the Red Cross, Thorvald Stoltenberg, who decided that the organization also should follow up with the inmates in the transition from imprisonment to society and make sure they were incorporated in the society. Estenstad was, in 2002, asked if he wanted to organize this work, later called "Network after Imprisonment." He accepted the offer, something he never regretted. He thinks he has the greatest and most meaningful job in the world, not only when he is with inmates and former inmates on a 14-day sailboat trip, but even in everyday life. Today we find this network in several cities in Norway, five cities in Denmark and one in Iceland. Some of what makes Norway stand out is that volunteer organizations can apply for support and get it, to assist former prisoners after their release. They then cooperate with the municipalities where the former prisoners live. Red Cross is only one of these organizations.

Cooperation in practice

In the middle of downtown Oslo, we find G26 Tilbakeføringssenter (Return Center), the new premises to Nettverk etter Soning where Estenstad works. It is the first one in Norway and for him it is a dream come true. For many years he has worked collecting important cooperators under one roof. The center is 2,000 square meters and it houses important agencies and other organizations which together help inmates with the transition from prison to society. Here we find a social office, the prison care, school services and a radio channel where convicts serve as radio converters. Nettverk etter soning has its own work training, volunteer mentors, activity possibilities and assisting family and youths. They also have debt counselling, and other sorts of counseling and assistance available for those coming here after their imprisonment.

Estenstad says,

> Our goal is that former inmates can walk in a door and get the best possible help for their different challenges. It is important for us to work for social inclusion and to ensure that they eventually can be able to get lasting work. We have education possibilities and work training and we offer social activities to former inmates and their families. To make sure that the inmates shall be included and feel safe we have about 250–300 volunteers and 15 employees. Their task is to follow up about 400 ex-convicts here in Oslo.

As a volunteer, one must be 25 years old, have a clean record and go through necessary courses and training in role understanding and security.

"This network has a lot of resources. In addition to young people under education who want work experience we have several retirees with broad expertise who work here," he continues. Estenstad knows that this special network means a lot for every single person.

He says that many of the former inmates actually get an offer of housing, work or school after their release. But if their colleagues, neighbors, or fellow students consider them former drug addicts and convicted prisoners it will be difficult for them. Even worse is perhaps that creditors will turn up and the mailbox will be filled up with debt-collection letters as soon as they get a place to live. Some of the participants experience that they can't even open a bank account.

Digital exclusion

The challenges that former prisoners meet when they are released can feel overwhelming. Society has gone through a digital transformation that is enormous. All the public-assistance systems like NAV, and health and social services, are digital, and for former inmates without any digital competence this barrier may feel extremely heavy when they are in need of housing and personal help after their release from prison. It is easier to manage at daytime than in the evening and weekends; so many former prisoners struggled with social anxiety and were isolated from the outside world. There is a great deal of social exclusion and Nettverk etter Soning wishes to catch this up and work for social integration.

Special cabins for families

For former inmates with family and children it can be difficult to be released from prison. It is not easy to tell your children that they cannot buy new clothes, participate in activities, or go on holidays because you are strained financially. How can you tell them without disappointing them too much? Estenstad sums up what this is all about in three short points:

1. Social anxiety
2. Social competence
3. Social status.

Estenstad says,

> Red Cross has cabins that families can use so they can spend time together. This is arranged through the network and the volunteers can bring their own families on a trip as well. It is very popular. Here they can enjoy outdoor life, boat trips and climbing trips and they play football as well.

Professional management of volunteering

Estenstad says,

What separates our work with volunteers from others is that we have professional management of the volunteers and organizations of this work. They are concerned with taking care of the former inmate while they also have in mind that our volunteers shall feel they are safe. We differentiate and discriminate because we know that people have different needs and challenges. The most important part of the job, and what makes us most happy, is to help the former inmates to get a job, a place to live, a good life and control of their economy. To succeed with that we must be able to see the individual person and his needs.

Estenstad is a man who is present in the conversation and makes everybody around aware that they are seen and listened to. He says that he has learnt a lot from Thorvald Stoltenberg, whom he describes as a charismatic leader who had the gift of giving everybody in the organization a sense of being important. He was present in the moment and made Estenstad believe it helps. He even gave him both a hug and a pat on the back. Estenstad seems slightly touched when he points at a big photo of his former boss hanging on the wall. "It was probably in his genes and Jens Stoltenberg (the current NATO chief) I think, has inherited much of that personality," he says.

Collaboration with business

Estenstad means that all things are connected, and he has been able to travel both in Norway and in other parts of the world to learn from others. He says that he is as good a thief as the raven and steals ideas from others when he travels around, because he thinks we can learn from each other when it concerns good criminal care both behind bars and in the work to include former convicts into society. He himself is engaged in getting Norwegian criminal care a coordinating responsibility in the Return Center and the establishment of similar centers in the largest cities. In his opinion, this should have been a public responsibility and not the responsibility of an NGO such as Red Cross.

The center already has a good dialogue with the prison and probation services about their role and how the cooperation with the center must be. Estenstad has worked for many years as a prison officer, and in the care of released prisoners, and has seen much good work done. He thinks the two groups together can help even more inmates and former prisoners with compound challenges.

He thinks that one of the toughest, most stigmatizing and most shameful challenges for many former convicts is the heavy burden of debt. They have therefore more than 50 volunteer advisers who can assist with advice in the center. In addition, Lindorff is running counseling courses on their premises for those who are interested. Many of the participants bring big plastic bags containing unopened envelopes with unpaid bills when they come. Red Cross says clearly that they will not take over this responsibility and the task belongs to the public sector.

"There are many other countries with better schemes for their inmates. In Polish prisons e.g., in addition to payment, they also earn a pension when they are imprisoned. After imprisonment they get a similar job. This makes the transition easier," Estenstad says. In Norway the inmates lose their pension when they are behind bars, and they often have private and public debt when they are outside. The center tries to encourage private companies to employ their participants. For the companies this is a good opportunity to show their social responsibility.

"It is important that work and education available in prisons and the time after is relevant and demanded," Estenstad says. He tells us about the Red Bike project, which is a bicycle workshop for both inmates and those released. It was established in partnership with Oslo Prison and pedagogic leaders inside the prison. A Red Bike bicycle workshop was established outside the prison in 2021. A new measure, New Network, has also been established to assist the youngest criminals from the ages of 15 to 22.

Another project is the company Hogst AS, which is a partnership between Red Cross and TrønderEnergi. It has been in operation for six years and provides work for ten former inmates. Here they learn to be manual forestry workers. This is one of the social construction projects the network runs in partnership with private business.

"Through social entrepreneurship we help people who have fallen outside society to get a new real possibility in line with FN's sustainability goals," Estenstad says.

Network is socioeconomically profitable

Estenstad says that even if they never had any thoughts around which savings the society could get from this work, there is a great economic advantage in this.

> We asked an insurance company to try to find out the saving there will be if our participants can manage in society. They should figure out what a person saves society if he or she becomes law-abiding after release. In a period of 20 years the savings for those who work will be at least NOK 15–21 million for each one of them. For those who receive social-security benefits there will be savings of at least NOK 10–15 million.

Estenstad says that a prison cell in a Norwegian high-security prison costs about NOK 2,700 per day.

While this survey was conducted, Network after Imprisonment had a daily price of NOK 72 for each participant.

"So, by investing in these people we save the society an enormous amount, and we will get a safer society."

Export product?

"We need increased resources for the prisons and repatriation work. I think we must prepare the inmates for a society in rapid change, especially concerning the digital transformation." He also means people have to work smarter and cooperate better, and that the public to a greater extent must be able to cooperate across different public sectors. FN's 17 sustainability goals and the green shift must include human resources (which have gone astray), not only the reuse of material resources and CO_2 emissions.

Estenstad says that the best part of his work is to see people turn from having been a burden to become a resource. "Social inclusion concerns us all," he states.

Recently the International Committee of the Red Cross (ICRC) asked Stian Estenstad to share his experiences in Norway. This is because the Red Cross in other countries, such as Ireland and Australia, is interested in doing something similar.

This is what Estenstad observes happens to those who participate:

1. They establish new and safe social networks
2. They get help to take control of their own private finances
3. They get an ordinary job
4. They manage to get out of heavy drug addiction
5. The become good parents for their children
6. They build self-confidence and a belief in themselves and the future.

This is the Red Cross's "Network after imprisonment"

The Red Cross's "Network after imprisonment" project is a measure that helps released who want to do something with their life situation. The risk of recidivism is greatest in the first year after release, and therefore a good support apparatus around the convict is important at this time and in the transition phase between imprisonment and release.

Network after imprisonment includes things like one-on-one follow-ups, social meeting places where the participants receive training in social skills, activities in their spare time, work training and help to get a job, assistance with debt and private finances, a special project for young ex-prisoners and an offer to the children of those who are convicted. Their goal is to provide the convicts an opportunity to increase their life skills and help them to establish a life which is not ruled by crime and drugs.

The network is now established in Oslo, Bergen, Stavanger, Trondheim, and Viken in Norway. The Danish government guarantees economic supply in a period of four years, but we have no such guarantee in Norway. Estenstad and his companions must search in every corner for funds to maintain and develop this activity. Today they receive financial support from the Norwegian prison and probation services, the Directorate of Health, the Environment Agency, the Police Directorate, the Directorate for Children, Youth and Family Affairs, NAV, municipalities, and businesses, foundations, and legacies.

> "As I walked out the door toward the gate that would lead to my freedom, I knew if I didn't leave my bitterness and hatred behind, I'd still be in prison."
>
> – *Nelson Mandela*

"Your choices. Your freedom. Your responsibility." These words are written on a discreet sign outside the Way Back's premises just by Oslo Cathedral in the middle of the capital of Norway. Downstairs we find Retretten (the Retreat), and upstairs the general manager, Johan Lothe, of Way Back Oslo invites us for lunch. This address is important because this is one of the places former inmates can meet and spend time together with friends, volunteers, and sponsors. A man with a pram comes in behind us and settles down to get himself a cup of coffee while his son runs around and chatters with the others. The atmosphere in the TV room is relaxed and there is no difference between volunteers, sponsors and visitors.

Like Retretten, which also was established by a former drug addict, Rita Nilsen, who struggled with starting a life without drugs, the foundation Way Back was established by a former inmate with drug addiction in 2002. Nowadays both foundations run under the same roof in Kristian August's street nr 10 in Oslo. According to Lothe, Way Back started as a project in Oslo Prison in 2001 so that convicts could have a life after release. Many former prisoners wondered why many who had served long drug sentences soon were back in prison after their release. So, the boys decided to do something to help each other on their way out of prison and wrote a letter to Are Høidal, the head of Oslo Prison. In that letter they said that they wanted to build an organization consisting of former prisoners to help each other to a life without drugs and crime. At the bottom of the letter it was clearly written that they understood that they themselves had to contribute to bring about a change. This was what made Høidal aware that they were serious, and he thought it was a good idea. He asked organizations outside prison care to form an organization. Kirkens Bymisjon and Tyrilistiftelsen were of good help when they started in 2002, but even today prison care is the most important partner in the nationwide foundation.

"Way Back has as its goal that former convicts are integrated in society and working life and through that manage to become active and responsible citizens," Lothe says and leads us through the kitchen and into the living room.

> Our motto is solidarity, friendship, and freedom from drugs, and by now we are established in the five biggest cities in Norway. We have many volunteers and about 16 sponsors who work

for us. What is special is that all sponsors themselves are convicts, and when you apply it is a good thing if you have been drug-addicted. To us it is as if you have an additional experience on your CV.

The sponsors start their work with inmates about half a year before they are released so they can come to know each other first. Lothe underlines that at this place all former convicts who have a residence permit are welcome regardless of conviction.

It is an important function that people can recognize themselves and learn from each other. Many struggle with social anxiety to come out in society, but in this place, it is like a safe haven, and they don't need to explain much. What is important is the will to change. They are the best for former inmates to build networks and social relations, and they can follow former inmates to meetings with the public such as NAV. They can have a conflict-reducing effect and make sure there is a good communication so the former convicts can make it clear what they really need help with.

Lothe says,

> We are not going to take over public responsibility, but we try to coordinate the different instances like NAV, educational institutions, doctors, and substance-abuse care. That makes the transition to freedom arranged for the individual on his or her own premises. We always used to remind people that they are the captain in their own life.

Thinks it's time for a new deposit report

The leader of Way Back tells that he had the great benefit of the more formal "Nettverk etter Soning," run by the Red Cross, when he was released after many years behind bars. He was the director who commuted between wife and children in Norway and business meetings throughout the continent. One day he became a drug addict and criminal and had himself heroin withdrawal when he ended up in prison. After five years behind bars convicted for drug-related law offenses, he can well recognize himself in those who come here. There is a lot of administrative work, but most of his job is to meet the released at the prison gate and stay with him for the first hours of freedom. A typical trip is to NAV to get money, perhaps keys to housing, then the grocery store and different department stores to buy a cell phone, linen, and kitchen utensils. Most of the released have no bank cards or ID and must pay with cash or a requisition from NAV.

Few know the problem

He sighs and says,

> I am surprised about how few people know the content in the separate report from the Civil Ombudsman from 2019 that cast a critical glance on conditions of imprisonment. It was about the use of belt bed, the lack of formal decision on such use, lack of supervision of security cell and general mental health among inmates in Norway today. Major deficiencies and unclear guidelines were discovered. The Minister of Health, Bent Høie, listened and agreed that a new supervisor was needed. Way Back is fortunately so well known that we are included in those advisings, and when we recently had a meeting with the Minister of Labor and the Minister of Health, we asked for a new penitentiary report. In the previous report neither the relatives nor the user's perspective were included.

He means that we in Norway have one of the best welfare systems in the world, but we need to work smarter and cooperate more across agencies. Today we have many important services like health and education and NAV, but they don't communicate and the inmate's mental health is not always taken care of.

He says,

> When people are imprisoned it is a unique possibility to get out a better product, because these are people who are present at school or at work every day, and they are free from drugs. Therefore is it important that this continues when they are released.

The increasing use of electronic control has resulted in that many of the resourceful inmates who contributed to calm down conflicts and who helped other inmates with support functions are gone. The result is that the prison is left with those who are not suitable for serving outside, and that means bigger problems but less people.

The Salvation Army assists inmates when they are released

The Salvation Army has worked with prisoners for more than 100 years. The manager of the Salvation Army's prison work in Norway, Yury Zelentsov, is especially proud of the program "Safe Way Home" established in 2008. The program assists inmates with an expulsion decision (i.e. inmates facing the possibility of being sent back to their home countries).
"Many are extremely vulnerable when they are going to be released and have perhaps just a tiny network in their homeland. We have then assisted them for up to three months with what they need, whether it is housing, contacts, or other things," Zelentsov says.

In Norway there are seven persons working full-time with this project. They cooperate with the Salvation Army or other organizations in the homeland of those they assist.

The Salvation Army works today in 133 countries. Zelentsov has worked at Trandum asylum reception[1] and has previous experience from helping victims of human trafficking and slavery.

"There are still victims of human trafficking in Norwegian prisons. They often have nothing, and we follow them up extra," he says. Even the Russian Zelentsov feels that he has the world's most meaningful job today.

Helped 154 people home

> Since we started this program, we have helped 154 people back to 51 different countries after they have served time in Norwegian prisons. Only five of these have returned illegally to Norway and three received a new verdict and were imprisoned again.

The Salvation Army works in more than 133 countries. That means that they have a worldwide network which can assist those who are released from Norwegian prisons with helping them to be picked up at the airport, finding housing, restoring contact with the family or establishing another positive network. Zelentsov says that many foreign inmates have more confidence in them than in prison staff.

He says,

> Many have basically a very negative attitude to the public authorities in their home countries. They see there is a mixing of roles in Norwegian prisons when the prison officers who engage in the exercise of power offer help and assist in the work towards their freedom. People are vulnerable and often they have complex challenges. For me it feels meaningful to listen to the stories behind the crimes they have committed.

84 Release to freedom – mind the gap

To be able to help people, the Salvation Army must start the process before they are released, so they may know that they have a will to change and even want the help.

The Norwegian project has found international recognition. Sometimes they receive requests from prisons in other countries asking if they can assist inmates. It varies how many they are able to help, but in 2022 they already work with 2–3 people, and they don't know how many there will be at the end.

Zelentsov says,

> Our work starts long before the prisoner is released. We talk and try to find out as much as possible to make life after imprisonment easier so they will choose another way. An inmate has to show that he is willing to change, and we can do much to make the transition to freedom and the journey back to their homeland as easy as possible.

During the pandemic it was difficult to make this work. That led to a steep decline from 33 Safe Way Home cases all over Norway in 2019 to only nine in 2020. The Correctional Service keeps no record of how the expelled foreigners were handled under the pandemic.

Other organizations that are important for the released and their family

The Prison Families Alliance (PFA) is another organization for the relatives of someone who is in custody, prison or in probation service. This is an organization that helps relatives and friends of Norwegian prisoners with advice regarding finances, social issues, community, applications and complaints, and about the situation of children and family. They also organize many social events and activities so that people are able to meet with others in the same situation. The service PFA offers is free of charge.

Note

1. Trandum asylum is the immigration detention center. Foreigners can be held in internment here.

17

LITTLE SCANDINAVIA AND OTHER INTERNATIONAL COLLABORATION

The Norwegian prison officer Line Syverstad and two of her colleagues are excited to visit a prison in the US for the first time. It is a big day for them, but also for the prison.

From the outside, Pennsylvania's State Correctional Institution at Chester (SCI Chester) looks like almost any other prison in the United States. But inside there are a lot of unique activities.

After a delay of more than two years due to the pandemic, the Little Scandinavia Unit will open. It is an important milestone for the Pennsylvania Department of Corrections, SCI Chester, and the officers who have been working for years to make their vision into reality.

Inspiration both ways

As we read earlier, Norway was inspired by a prison in Philadelphia when they built the first prison in Oslo[1] in 1851.[2] Now, in May 2022, inspiration has gone in the opposite direction. A unit in SCI Chester, the first of its kind, is ready to take care of prisoners the Scandinavian way.

The effort to open a Scandinavia-inspired prison unit began in 2017. Are Høidal, governor at Halden Prison, visited SCI Chester to speak about the Norwegian approach to incarceration.[3] After that, and with the approval of then-Secretary of Corrections John Wetzel, a collaboration was developed between the Pennsylvania Department of Corrections (PA DOC), the Norwegian Correctional Service (Kriminalomsorgen), the Swedish Prison and Probation Service (Krimnalvården), and the Danish Prison and Probation Service (Kriminalforsorgen). In the summer of 2019, a delegation from Pennsylvania that included frontline officers and leaders spent weeks in Scandinavian countries. During that time, the full group visited prisons, halfway houses, and the correctional college to learn, firsthand, about the systems and goals.[4] They focused their efforts on really understanding the way that the principle of normality,[5] a key ideal in Norway, was put into practice,[6] and how to create a different climate for officers and inmates.[7] The correctional officers spent weeks working side by side with Norwegian mentor officers at Ila, Ringerike, and Romerike prisons. After some pandemic-related delays, the team, along with new officers who joined the project, traveled to Sweden in the spring of 2022 to learn more. They were able to refine and refresh their understandings of Scandinavian penal principles by visiting Kumla, a maximum-security prison, and the training academy, among other events.

DOI: 10.4324/9781003195887-17

PHOTO 17.1 From left to right: Patricia Connor-Council, Jordan Hyatt, Synøve N. Andersen, Malin Anette Klund, Tina Olsen and Line Syverstad

Source: Photo: Nina Hanssen

Teamwork to create the Little Scandinavia Unit

The team from SCI Chester (USA), with the support of a research team led by Drexel University (USA) and the University of Oslo (Norway), have been working to develop the policies for this new unit since 2019. They have named this unit "Little Scandinavia." In this process, they received guidance from academics, psychologists, architects, and their Scandinavian peers, among others. Major construction and renovations began at that time too. As early as March 2020, six men sentenced to serve life in prison moved to the "Little Scandinavia" unit, but the completion of the project and the opening ceremony were delayed due to the pandemic.

Exchanging experiences

In May of 2022, both the inmates and the prison officers are excited. Among the visitors is Syverstad and her Norwegian colleagues. They are here to share their experiences from the Norwegian prison service with the SCI Chester and Little Scandinavia community. A documentary film team from Sweden's Television Stock Company (SVT) is filming and the research team, led by Jordan M. Hyatt, JD PhD, (Drexel University) and Synøve N. Andersen, PhD, (University of Oslo), is taking notes and is busy completing interviews with staff and inmates for its research about this unique project.

A total makeover

The unit manager for Little Scandinavia in the USA is Patricia Connor-Council, also called CC. She is welcoming her Norwegian colleagues. She is emotional and overwhelmed now that they are finally officially opening their unit and that more inmates will move in. CC has been on both trips to Scandinavia and is excited to try out some of the principles here in Chester. While we are walking through the corridors with colorful murals made by inmates, she tells us that there are huge differences between the "normal" units in the prison and the brand new unit that she and the officers have designed. In her unit, they have "contact officers" for the prisoners and a lot of interaction between employees and inmates. There is more staff per inmate than anywhere else, something they learned and adapted from Norway.

Heartfelt reunion with their families

There are tears and laughter during the opening ceremony, as well as many positive emotions in the unit. The first six residents of Little Scandinavia also had an exciting day. They were encouraged to invite a family member to attend the opening ceremony. Today their family members are sitting next to their incarcerated loved ones and are interspersed throughout the audience. After the ceremony, the family members also have an opportunity to visit the unit. For most of the men, this is the first time that a family member sees where they live while incarcerated. CC says that this shows how this project fosters a heightened sense of human dignity. And she is excited to work in an environment that creates "normality" and "dynamic security" to effect rehabilitation and success outside the walls of SCI Chester. This gives hope for the future, she says.

By the end of the summer of 2022, the Little Scandinavia Unit will have a lot more inmates and several dedicated officers working there.

"I have a dream," CC says. Her dream is that all the 14 units in this prison will follow the Scandinavian principle and work differently.

"What if we can manage to inspire more prisons in Pennsylvania and then over the whole of USA?" she says while she is guiding her visitors around. CC is proud of her officers who have really made a change and are doing a great job. The physical changes to "Little Scandinavia," which are dramatic when compared to a regular unit, were almost complete just before COVID-19 changed everything.

Single cells for everyone

Among the physical changes is that inmates were moved from double cells to single cells. The prisoners also have access to a new commercial kitchen with stoves, microwave ovens and big fridges they can use if they want to make their own food. There is a landscaped outdoor area just for these inmates. The furniture in the common areas and the cells was designed for this unit. This is the only unit in Pennsylvania with these features.

"I believe moving from double-bunking to single-bunking in all cells means a lot for the prisoners," CC says. As we walk into the unit there is yellow soft seating throughout, and they have game tables in the common area. In the middle of the open room there is a reflection area that includes a large fish tank. Little Scandinavia also has an outdoor green space for residents of the unit. They have also developed a grocery program that allows residents to budget for and order groceries from a community-based supermarket. CC believes this will make life easier for both her staff but also for the inmates. Increasing the quality of life universally is an important goal for everyone on the project. Dr. Marayca Lopez I. Ferrer, among others, has advised the SCI Chester team for the changes to the physical design of this prison. She is also excited on the opening day and we meet her sitting down with some of the residents in the soft chairs.

Beyond the physical spaces

The changes go beyond the physical spaces. With the permission of the PA DOC leadership, the Little Scandinavia officers have revised the guidelines to make it easier for them to implement new routines that will encourage interactions between employees and inmates.

PHOTO 17.2 The unit manager for Little Scandinavia in the USA is Patricia Connor-Council, photographed in this picture with justice planner Dr. Marayca Lopez, who provided guidance during the exploration of unit upgrades with a focus on creating a normalized environment

Source: Photo: Nina Hanssen

All the prison officers and residents have different uniforms than those working and living in the rest of the prison. Moreover, the Little Scandinavia officers have worked to revise policies on important topics to reflect what they learned in Scandinavia, including:

- Discipline
- Uniforms for incarcerated people

PHOTO 17.3 The Norwegian prison officer Line Syverstad outside SCI Chester
Source: Photo: Nina Hanssen

- Dining options
- Commissary privileges
- Visitation
- Reentry planning.

CC feels grateful for being part of this new project and she says that the restructured fraternization policy is particularly exciting as it permits and encourages a whole new range of interactions between staff and incarcerated persons.
"This is the heart of the intervention," she says.

Permanent or just a project?

"This is a fantastic project, and I really hope it will last for more than two years, so that they can be able to measure recidivism," Line Syverstad says as we walk through the green areas. She is the responsible prison officer for department F in Ila Detention and Security Prison outside of Oslo.

What is your impression of how American prisons are run and how your American colleagues work in practice?

> My experience is that professionals in American prisons want to and try to make meaningful choices, but the job is difficult because of organizational circumstances. Among other things, officers can be terminated on behalf of what I consider necessary and professional relations with imprisoned people. My impression is that American prisons facilitate dynamic security, where relationship skills are emphasized, only to a small degree. Further, it must be highlighted that Norwegian prison officers are increasingly more educated and for that reason have more formal qualifications to theoretically anchor their choices and actions in their professional practice.

Asking Syverstad about the biggest difference between Norwegian and American prison services, she replies:

> The greatest difference from a prison officer's view is that resources and competence are different when it comes to working with inmates to help them change attitudes and make them prepared for a life outside prison. I am not sure what tools the prisoners in USA can work on so that they can manage to break out of their criminal pattern of action. And then it is a great difference that inmates in American prisons often serve their sentences in double cells and there is even a window in the cell doors. The prisoners also have limited physical contact with their relatives. Furthermore, inmates in Norwegian prisons have the same rights as the other residents in Norway. As I have understood the inmates in American prisons are deprived of their rights, such as the right to vote.

Cooperative learning

Syverstad find the Little Scandinavia Unit important because the exchange of experiences provides an opportunity to reflect on how both Americans and we in Norway practice the execution of sentences. "Cooperative learning" means that tasks are broken up, and that individuals are given the responsibility for parts of the common work. "Collaborative learning" is based on a collaborative perspective where discussion and reflection around a task or an issue are emphasized. Discussion creates a reflection that expands different perspectives on possible courses of action.

What can we Norwegian prison officers learn from American colleagues?

> What I have learned in this project is that inmates in USA, to a greater extent, must themselves ask to facilitate for their own imprisonment. I experienced the Little Scandinavia as more independent, partly digitally, since they had access to buy a tablet computer so they, themselves, could have contact with the outside world by e-mail, download music, and have access to their own account. This is in line with the principle of normality, as I see it. Further, I experienced that my American colleagues on the project radiated professional pride and were willing to see solutions with the cooperation with the Scandinavia that has started, despite experiencing resistance from colleagues. They gave prisoners trust by, among other things, letting them have access to a selection of knives in the kitchen. The knives were kept in locked cabinets and the knives could be secured by wire to the kitchen counter when needed. The inmate himself had the responsibility to sign up to the kitchen at any given time. That inspired us to look beyond our existing practices. Exchanges like this provide inspiration, create reflection and generate innovation for us too.[8]

A more humane prison environment

As we have heard, there is a lot cooking in Chester. And in addition to all the physical changes of the prison environment and practice, the Scandinavian Prison Project, a research project managed by Dr. Synøve N. Andersen (University of Oslo) and Dr. Jordan Hyatt (Drexel University), seeks to empirically assess what happens when certain practices and principles from Scandinavian corrections are implemented in an American prison setting. Andersen, who also gave a presentation during the opening ceremony, said that the close connection between reform and evaluation is one of the unique features of this project. Andersen and Hyatt are excited to be able to observe and get more experience about what happens when ideas and principles from Scandinavian corrections are implemented in other penal, social and cultural settings.

"Will these 'penal transplants' thrive in their new environment, or will we observe some unexpected responses and outcomes?" she asked the audience during the opening ceremony. She believes that the answers are relevant to all who are interested in comparative approaches to punishment and incarceration, including our partners in Scandinavia.

High expectations

The project in Chester is one of the many ongoing collaborations between the Norwegian Correctional Service, and prison and probation services abroad. Before the opening ceremony, Kim Ekhaugen, director of international cooperation in the Norwegian Correctional Service, praised the project, adding that he was impressed by the work so far. Ekhaugen looks forward to following the next phase of the project. Acting Secretary Little was also excited by this project and said that their vision is to create a more humane prison environment, including a dramatic shift in how staff and the incarcerated population interact.

"This reform will allow everyone living and working on the unit to focus on reintegration into society in a substantial way," he said.

In his address, Dr. Jordan Hyatt said that the unique combination of staff-developed training, policy updates, and physical design changes to the unit make this an important project with the potential to reshape how we approach corrections in Pennsylvania and beyond. And he added that by reimagining what incarceration looks like and focusing on rehabilitation rather than punishment, we have the potential to reduce recidivism and improve community outcomes.[9]

The Little Scandinavia Unit changed everything for Joe

He is sentenced to life in prison and has so far been imprisoned for 31 years after killing a man. Joseph Spinks was one of six men who moved into the Little Scandinavia Unit in 2020.

"Now I finally feel like a human being again," he says when we meet him the day after the official opening. Joseph, also called Joe, had a visit from his mother yesterday. He is still happy and admits it was a very emotional meeting.

> My mum has come to visit me all these years I have been imprisoned, but she has never been allowed inside the prison itself. She has only been in the visitor room with all the restrictions. Yesterday she, for the first time, was allowed to spend the day with me, have dinner with me, hug me and sit in the cell with me. Finally, she got peace in her soul. Now she knows I´m fine.

Life imprisonment is common for serious crimes in the USA. In some states they still have the death penalty. Joe regrets his deeds but believe he has undergone a major change while in prison.

"I did something stupid in my youth and got my punishment. It is hard to be locked up. The food in American prisons is awful, we share a room with others, and there is almost no activity for us," he says. Joe looks around his "new" Scandinavian home and smiles.

"The advantage of bad food is that I l have lost weight," he says as he points at the lunch of the day which lays on the table in front of us. Here in the Little Scandinavia Unit the inmates can make their own food and he will do that today.

"You can take this away," he says to his contact officer Devane, and pats himself jokingly on the stomach. Devane, who has worked in this prison for four years, smiles at Joe and gives his shoulder a friendly tap. She thrives here and enjoys the good relations between people. Here, the prison officers have other rules than in the rest of the prison, and dynamic security and good relations between employees and inmates is the core of the scheme.

PHOTO 17.4 Prisoner Joe Spinks was one of six men who moved into the Little Scandinavia Unit in 2020. His contact officer, prison officer Devane, really enjoys the new way of working

Source: Photo: Nina Hanssen

Before she was transferred to work in the Little Scandinavia Unit, Devane worked in other units with a lot of isolation, an issue that bothers her a lot. Some inmates sit in isolation for an indefinite time and that is not good for their mental and physical health, she says. Prison officer Devane has, since she was very young, dreamt of working in prison care and has always been engaged in prison reform. She is proud of her profession but admits that American prison services have a long way to go before they are as humane as the Scandinavians'. She admires the good values and the practices in the Norwegian prisons, as well as the prison-officer education "Norwegians handle inmates with respect, and I was lucky to visit several Norwegian prisons in 2019," she says.

"Here the employees treat us as human beings, with respect, and not like animals. I feel dignity here," Spinks replies with a twinkle in his eye as he walks to the kitchen. He is optimistic about the future. "I feel blessed because I was chosen to be here in 'Little Scandinavia.' It is a calmer atmosphere here, it is cleaner, and we can talk more with fellow inmates and the employees about common things. It is more normal," he says.

The collaboration with Amend in US

Another collaboration is between KDI and Amend, sponsored by public and private donors in the United States.

Tom Eberhardt is the coordinator from the Norwegian Correctional Services. Amend is a project organization at the Criminal Justice and Health Program at the University of California, San Francisco. Although American delegations have visited Norwegian counterparts frequently since 2015, formal cooperation were entered into in 2019 when the parties signed a five-year agreement. In the US, the project is led by Professor Brie Williams. Amend's (formerly JUST Innovate) partners from Norway include KRUS and a number of prisons including Halden, Ila and Bredtveit, but also Oslo Transitional Housing and the Norwegian Directorate of Correctional Services.

In the United States, the partners are the states of California, Oregon, Washington, and North Dakota (May 2022). Previously involved states: Alaska, Hawaii, Idaho, Rhode Island, and New York.

According to Kim Ekhaugen, who is leading the international effort, the goal of this project is to reform prisons and to change the culture in American prisons to reduce the harmful health effects it has on staff and inmates. He says a distinctive aspect of Amend's work is the focus on the health of employees and especially on the health of prison officers. According to Ekhaugen, US prison officers are heavily overrepresented in a number of negative statistics on health challenges compared to other comparable occupational groups. The target group for the collaborative project is prison employees, politicians, bureaucrats, private investors and administrative staff inside and outside the justice sector. He says that so far, they have good results, and several states can point to impactful stories from inmates who have been affected by the cultural change in prison staff.

Great and inspiring cooperation

Autumn Engstrøm works for the North Dakota Department of Corrections and Rehabilitation. She is a case manager, which is a cross between a prison officer and a social worker. Her department has been collaborating with Amend for a while so the concepts aren't entirely new to her. She is now happy to be part of the ambassador program and in 2022 she visited several prisons in Norway, including Halden Prison.

What did you learn from your visit to the land of Vikings?

Autumn Engstrøm says,

> I learned the importance of humanity and teamwork in all decisions and operations. Not only for those living in prisons, but those also working in the prisons as well. Also collaboration with the community is very important. I believe this kind of international collaboration is important because we all can learn from each other and take things away to create the best possible systems in our own corners of the world to accomplish the goal of humanity and change.

She said they have changed a lot about North Dakota's prison culture.
"It was just really fantastic to see it all in person and have conversations with people in Norway."[10]

Correctional collaborations in Eastern Europe

In addition to the projects in the US, there are also ongoing collaborations between the Norwegian Correctional Service, and prison and probation services in several Eastern European countries. The Agreement on the European Economic Area (EEA) is the cornerstone of relations between Norway and the EU. The EEA Agreement brings together the 27 EU member states and the three EEA Efta states, Norway, Iceland and Liechtenstein, in the internal market governed by the same basic rules.

The starting point also for EEA funds is the EEA agreement – which is the main foundation of Norway's cooperation with the EU. The EEA Agreement includes a common goal with the EU to reduce social and economic inequalities in Europe. The second goal is to strengthen the donor countries' bilateral relations with the countries that receive support. The EEA funds are also an important tool in Norwegian foreign policy, which protect Norwegian interests and bilateral cooperation in areas with common challenges. Norway's focus areas address common European challenges, including growth/innovation and jobs, climate challenges and well-functioning justice systems/rule of law/migration. In this way, we make ourselves relevant not only in each individual recipient country, but also in relation to the EU.

Support for the justice sector and civil society has become increasingly important, as a result of the rule of law and democracy being under pressure in several countries in Europe today. The priority sector's Justice and Home Affairs aims at strengthening European citizens' confidence in their governments' ability to ensure civil rights, equal treatment and protection.

Correctional-service projects

Norway has an EEA project in seven countries:[11] Latvia, Lithuania, Czech Republic, Poland, Romania, Bulgaria and Croatia. The overall objective of correctional and probation services is development towards the standards of the Universal Declaration of Human Rights, the Standard Minimum Rules for the Treatment of Prisoners (the Nelson Mandela Rules[12]), European Court of Human Rights,[13] European Committee for the Prevention of Torture and Inhuman or Degrading Treatment or Punishment (CPT)[14] and European prison rules.

Typical challenges in these countries are overcrowded prisons, lack of services for the inmates, too little space in terms of area, poor food and hygiene, lack of health services, and lack of services for vulnerable groups. The goals and focus on the projects is to improve prison conditions through a combination of soft and hard measures:

- Construction of new prisons, halfway houses, renovation and new equipment
- Strengthen the competence of both prisoners and staff
- Build new training centers and improve the training and competence of staff
- Less crowded prisons
- Promote alternatives to prison: restorative justice, electronic monitoring and community service
- Activities for prisoners, school, work training, rehabilitation programs and leisure activities
- Strengthen focus on vulnerable groups.

Norway has over 20 partners from various prison and probation units who work actively in the projects. These units are partners with one recipient country. All countries aim to develop competence, as well as the University College of Norwegian Correctional Service. These collaborations have been subject to little empirical and academic scrutiny, and the extent to which "penal transplants" derived from the Scandinavian models may thrive outside their respective social and institutional contexts remains poorly understood.

Notes

1. Rubin, A. T. (2021). *The deviant prison: Philadelphia's Eastern state penitentiary and the origins of America's modern penal system, 1829–1913*. Cambridge: Cambridge University Press.
2. www.sixnorwegianprisons.com/ideas#:~:text=1851&text=Osloper cent 20Botsfengselper cent 20 (1851per cent 2D2017), by per cent 20prisonsper cent 20inper cent 20Pennsylvaniaper cent 2C per cent 20USA.
3. www.inquirer.com/philly/news/crime/coming-from-norway-pennsylvanias-prisons-appear-cruel-and-unusual-20171004.html
4. Hyatt, J. M., Andersen, S. N., Chanenson, S. L., Horowitz, V., & Uggen, C. (2021). "We Can Actually Do This": Adapting Scandinavian correctional culture in Pennsylvania. *American Criminal Law Review, 58*, 1715.
5. www.kriminalomsorgen.no/informasjon-paa-engelsk.536003.no.htm
6. Chanenson, S. L., Andersen, S. N., Hyatt, J. M., Hoidal, A., Eason, K., & Connor-Council, P. (2021). "Ice in the Stomach": Reforming prisons at home and abroad. *American Criminal Law Review, 58*, 1775.
7. Ibid.
8. Documentary on the Little Scandinavia. (196) Prison Project: Little Scandinavia (extended trailer) – YouTube.
9. The research project was made possible by grants from Arnold Ventures and the Nordic Research Council for Criminology. Read more about the projects from the research team here: www.nsfk.org/blog/the-scandinavian-prison-project-what-happens-when-scandinavian-correctional-principles-and-practices-travel-to-the-us/; www.insidehighered.com/quicktakes/2022/03/16/looking-scandinavia-american-prison-reform-academic-minute
10. Personal communication with Autumn Engstrøm 17.05.2022.
11. Correctional Services | EEA Grants.
12. Nelson Mandela Rules (unodc.org).
13. https://hudoc.echr.coe.int/eng
14. European Committee for the Prevention of Torture and Inhuman or Degrading Treatment or Punishment (CPT) (coe.int).

18
A PEEK INTO THE FUTURE

It is difficult to predict the future, but in correctional services as elsewhere in society, a digital transformation is in progress. Technology is changing our habits, our free time, and our working life. Many people organize their lives through smartphones and use other smart gadgets such as vacuum cleaners, robotic lawnmowers, and other technical aids to make everyday life easier. Throughout the pandemic, many have worked from home via computers and perhaps had the feeling of being isolated from the world. For many inmates in prisons around the world, this period has also been particularly difficult because they have spent more time alone in their cell, because the visitor schemes have been limited due to the risk of infection.

Digital visits

In order for the inmates to see and chat with their loved ones, iPad/reading boards were purchased that were security-cleared and handed out in some prisons.

In Norway, several prisons were closed to visitors and external actors, so the Correctional Services had to rethink and use technology at a much faster pace than they had prepared for.

There are other external things, too, that will affect the future of correctional services. In the Norwegian Correctional Services' business strategy for 2021–2026,[1] the agency has identified the strongest impetus that will affect them. Politically, there are changes and priorities in the police, as well as unforeseen situations and incidents with a major impact such as less economic room for change and a need for efficiency improvements. In addition, a more digital society and new technology will affect penal execution and reversal. The new "Punishment that changes" vision replaces the long-standing vision "Active correctional services – a safer community." It also emphasizes the values that employees will take with them further into the future, namely openness, security and innovation. The Norwegian Correctional Services have great ambitions in Norway, and they do place great demands on human rights. Among other things, the Correctional Services must reduce the use of isolation that is harmful, especially for vulnerable inmates.

There are still many old and outdated prisons in Norway, which were built during a time (the 19th century) where community and motivation were not so highly focused. This has been put much more on the agenda in recent years, with the European Prison Rules adopted by the Council of Europe's Committee of Ministers, and the Mandela Rules (UN Standard Minimum Rules for the Treatment of Prisoners). In Norway, there will be a focus in the future on getting prisons ready to satisfy the international rules in relation to motivation and outdoor time for the inmates. This requires architectural changes, but Norway is set to take action in all prisons that are in operation.

More than ever before, inmates act out and display violent behavior during the penal execution and this puts more pressure on the staff. The proportion of foreign inmates and convicts is decreasing, while the proportion of women in prison is increasing. The trend is also that there are more elderly convicts, which will mean more challenges related to treatment and care services for inmates. There has been a significant increase in the number of inmates convicted of sexual offences, and the Correctional Services must pay special attention to sex offenders in the high-risk recidivism group. Much of this crime is committed online.[2]

But how has the Correctional Service itself exploited the possibilities in relation to technology without compromising the safety and content of the sentence?

More inmates choose e-monitoring (EM)

During the pandemic, there was a 32% decrease in the number of people carrying out their sentences in prison, and an 8% increase in those who carried them out with electronic monitoring (EM).[3] Today, there are more convicts who carry out their punishment in the public community than in prison. The introduction of electronic monitoring (ankle bracelets) is the main reason for this. The advantage of this is, among other things, that the convict avoids a break in study or work. At the same time, they can also maintain close ties with family and friends. For this type of punishment, it is important that this does not become an additional burden on communities or others. In Norway, the probation office is responsible for this punishment. The probation service is an included part of the correctional services. The new digital control measures provide increased security for society because one knows where the convicts are always, and there are few relapses among those serving sentences with ankle bracelets. This kind of thing frees up prison capacity and resources. Ankle monitoring normalizes imprisonment by reducing the threshold for returning to a normal, law-abiding life. The paradox here is that in Norway there are many open prisons with low levels of control, and e-monitoring will have a higher degree of control than what is found in some open prisons, where tougher criminals are.

Seamless correctional services

In the business strategy of the Correctional Services for 2021–2026, it is stated "that the convicts shall face a seamless prison care where they interact across criminal execution in prisons and society, ensuring equal treatment and legal security for all".[4] There is a clear goal that they should have a timely and secure digital practice and use new technology both for learning and in repatriation work.

Digital self-service prison

In the midst of the pandemic in 2020, Norway opened a large and modern prison in Agder that would use technology in a way no one had tried before. Agder Prison, department Mandal was to be a more modern version of Halden Prison.

The prison in Agder is much like a traditional prison on the outside with high fences and many security measures. However, when you enter, you quickly understand that this is a very modern prison with many smart solutions. This prison is the most modern we have in Norway and has been referred to as the prison of the future. At the entrance, they have already put in place the new modern body scanners that are reminiscent of those used in the security check at the airport. In several Norwegian prisons, visitors and inmates must pass through these scanners before being allowed in.

PHOTO 18.1 New Agder prison in Mandal
Source: Photo: Kriminalomsorgen

There is still a discussion going on about the suitability of these machines to prevent the smuggling of drugs into the prison. The goal was to have fewer physical body searches, to make the prison more accessible to visitors and lawyers, and to avoid inhuman invasions of body openings. While it may facilitate the work of the employees, many people are concerned that they do not uncover everything that may be hidden in body openings.

But the prison leader in Agder Prison, Frank M. Tveiten Johansen, believes this is a good supplement and is very proud to lead one of the world's most digital prisons. He tells about all the gadgets on the walls and roofs and the equipment the prison has invested in to test new technology in sentencing. At the same time, he emphasizes that in Norwegian correctional services, employees will always be the most important resource for the inmates. Several cuts in correctional services over the years have made everyday life tougher for prison managers, and that leads to harsh priorities.

Breath and movement shells

To make everyday life easier for employees, the prison has installed several cells with a breath and motion sensor, to support the consideration of whether to intervene. There's some kind of surveillance device on the ceiling that checks that the inmate is breathing. This can prevent overdoses and suicides, which is still a problem in Norwegian prisons. An alarm goes off if you do not move or breathe for ten seconds. This is not only life-saving, but also labor-saving. Where employees otherwise walk around and physically check that the inmates are breathing, they now get help from modern technology. The sensor is white and looks like a shell.

But still, the prison officers are our most important asset, according to the director.

Cashless

The future prison will be completely contactless, and the intention is that the inmates shall serve themselves food via computer screens in common areas or via tablets. When we visited the prison a few months after the opening, not all the digital devices were in the space yet, but the wall-mounted kiosk hung clear. During 2021, the employees used the system 210 times in connection with visits. The system uses bank ID through mobile devices, so that one secures the identities of those who wish to visit.

To meet the digital challenges and become more seamless, correctional services are transitioning from the old data system and introducing KODA version 1.0, which is a forward-looking IT tool where two-way communication becomes easier. Today, inmates can use the platform for requests, internal messages, notice boards and activity planners, but within a short time it will also be possible to use the system to read messages from relatives, organize visits, and order food.

An inmate we talked to missed his time in the previous prison where they were given ready-made food, but most of all he missed his freedom. So did everyone we met around the common table. No one seemed particularly excited about the situation, and that is perhaps understandable. The time in prison with extra restrictions due to the pandemic is tough.

Self-catering means they have to cook all the food themselves inside the prison. They have a modern shop inside the prison, where there is a good atmosphere and where the inmates work. The store is at a high level in terms of service and has a range of goods that can be fully compared to a regular food store outside the walls. For some, this works very well, if they benefit from a modern and nice kitchen and good ingredients, but for inmates without the ability to take care of themselves, it is a challenge. An inmate complained that he only ate straight-in-the-cup for months, because the challenge of cooking his own healthy food became too great.

He told me he'd never loved being in the kitchen. The food he eats is very one-sided and he eats just noodles. He was looking forward to them being able to order pizza on the digital screen.

An American inmate believed that prison in Norway was much better than at home in the United States. Another of the inmates complained that there were so few offers of schooling and work during the day.

A university graduate who had been a leader for many years wondered what he was going to do with forklift certificates or carpentry. Now they only received schooling offers at the upper secondary level. It would be much better if they were given the opportunity for further education at a university level or at least online courses, he said. A teacher from the local high school broke in. He understood that some meant the school system could have improved and said he should see what he could do. The online possibilities are huge, but security clearance is important.

Today, no one is allowed to use a cell phone in Norwegian prisons and internet access is limited. The inmates in Agder sighed. They felt they had missed the new digital everyday life that many people have outside the walls. A statistic of what the inmates used the messaging services for in 2021 shows that most of the messages went to the health department.

Own bank cards

Soon the inmates in this prison will have their own bank ID linked to cards that can be used both inside the prison and in the wider community on leave. They are looking forward to this and they especially think it is a good idea that those closest to them can then top them up with some extra money via the Vipps app. This will soon become possible, it is a unique situation and perhaps only possible because Norway is a society where money transactions are recorded. If there is a larger amount, they must notify where this is coming from. Many inmates do not have to deal with personal finances during prison sentences. Therefore, the transition becomes enormous when they are released and again must deal with bank cards and other digital services. For many released, obtaining a bank account can also be challenging. We've all heard of inmates getting out and no longer being able to pay for themselves on the bus home, because the bus companies have switched to mobile payment solutions. Norwegian society is now so technologically developed that you can hardly do anything without apps, logins and bank IDs. Getting this technology into the prisons gives the inmates an important competence that makes them more prepared for life on the outside. The more prison life resembles life outside the walls, the easier it will be to handle life on the day you get out. This is the essence of the concept of normality that is so central to modern Norwegian correctional thinking.

In Agder Prison in Mandal, they have therefore adopted digital payment solutions and received their own bank cards that can be used both inside and outside the prison. Then family and friends can easily transfer money to the inmate if he or she needs something extra.

The inmates will get more digital games and maybe their own tablets. There are high expectations among both inmates and staff, and they are looking forward to all the screens being fully used to communicate. Here they will soon be able to send messages, check the activity calendar, talk to relatives and in the future order meals, play games and watch videos. The new digital solution will offer better and coordinated information about activities. Registration of activity may be automated, including payment of salary. Digitalization may make inmates more self-reliant, but for many an update of knowledge about digital solutions is needed. Perhaps they should be offered courses on how to become a "digital citizen"? Either way, both the prison manager and the staff are very excited about what this will be like.

More activities

They hope that digitalization will lead to an increased degree of self-motivation in the evenings and weekends, such as self-study and the use of library services. It will be easier to offer an e-learning platform, both for employees and inmates. The exception is inmates who take education courses while in prison. They may have limited and controlled access to the internet for teaching purposes.

Almost the only thing the inmates were unhappy with was the supply of work. These included forklift driver's certificates, carpentry, a shop job or school offers in upper secondary school. Leisure facilities were varied, from gaming to sports activities and artistic pursuits, but many still felt that it did not suit their interests. Ultimately, the quality of closed prisons is about how large the number of staff who can follow up with the inmates is. A closed prison will always have limited opportunities to provide inmates with services both in terms of leisure activities and further education. Digital solutions will only make things easier for the inmates and staff, but the number of heads, hearts and hands is what really matters. No technology can fully replace human contact, not even in a prison – yes, perhaps this is extra important to keep in mind in a prison where many can easily be left alone with bad thoughts and feelings.

Human contact

The goal of the IT solution is thus to strengthen communication and not remove the value of direct human contact between staff and inmates.

E-incarceration/electronic monitoring (EM)

As mentioned earlier, there are now more convicts in Norway who carry out punishments in society than in prison. Electronic monitoring (through ankle bracelets) is the main reason for this. It's an easier sentence for many since it allows them to continue their lives seemingly without major changes. They can go to work and school, and the detention involves only control and restrictions in their free time. There are currently clear conditions for being granted an e-incarceration. You must not be convicted of serious crimes, such as terrorism, aggravated violence, and sexual assault of minors. To get an e-incarceration, you must have some form of housing, and a job or study, and you have to apply for it yourself. In 2021, there were 3,691 convictions with an ankle bracelet. Most stay at home while they serve their sentence. The sentences are on average 92 days. A relevant criticism of electronic monitoring is that it is a form of prison that only the most resourceful convicts can carry out as it requires, among other things, an orderly private life where their own dwelling or apartment is necessary. The least resourceful inmates don't have this. Another objection, which was, among other things, the main criticism of this form of imprisonment from former Minister of Justice Odd Einar Dørum (Human Party), is that by serving with ankle bracelets (or foot shackles as the opponents call it), the home is turned into a prison. Whether it's okay with the convict is one thing, whether it's just as well if the convict lives with someone, such as a girlfriend or child, is another matter.

The tracking technology gives the Correctional Services various possibilities. Depending on what the verdict says, the electric monitor can be put on passive, active or hybrid. This activates it when you get home (passive), when you're in a place you're not supposed to be (hybrid) or at all times (active).

Major change in recent years

In 2020, the average time of imprisonment increased from four months to six, which means that those convicted of violence have also to some extent been given an e-incarceration. The technology allows for tracking people 24 hours a day. In England, they have also been granted permission to track inmates after completing their sentences, for up to a year. We have not come that far in Norway. It would have been a[5] direct violation of privacy and the principle that one has served the sentence when released from prison.

While e-incarceration can work well for those with a functioning family around them, for others it can mean more loneliness and isolation. Basic preliminary examinations should be carried out to determine whether this form of imprisonment may be worth using. The Norwegian Prison and Probation Officers' Union (NFF) has always demanded that if ankle bracelets are to be used, they must have meaningful content for the convicted person as well. It must not only become a form of detention, but a prison service with contact between the convicted and prison employees. The first man to serve his sentence with EM with GPS tracking in Norway said he would have preferred prison over the ankle bracelet. To him prison means less freedom, but it wasn't that bad since you have someone to talk to all the time. After a week, prison is perceived as everyday life, he meant. New technology means that the Correctional Service not only has control over where the person who has an ankle bracelet stays at all times, but a video solution has also been established for convicts with ankle bracelets (video in communities, a conversation tool and a supplement to physical meetings). It can also be an alternative to unannounced checks in your home or at work. A trial scheme allows the person serving with an ankle bracelet to be called via a locked smartphone that will only be used for this purpose. The person in question is then asked to insert a tube similar to the ones we are asked to breathe into during random traffic checkpoints, to see if alcohol has been drunk. Those sitting at the other end of the video call can ensure through facial recognition or fingerprints (biometrics) that convicts take the alcohol test, without having to scramble and disturb him or her in their everyday life. This is carried out every week or every two weeks, depending on what the judge has decided. In the case of a positive result, you take another test after 20 minutes. If the test is positive, you risk having to serve a further sentence in a normal prison.

Inmates who do not live alone think video solutions are better than the police suddenly showing up at your door. These digital control measures are also possible to use for ordinary inmates who are going on leave, release or parole. Sweden was the first Nordic country to introduce this form of prison. It quickly showed good results and has been interesting for both Norwegian and Danish correctional services.

According to the Correctional Services, there are many advantages to using new technology in sentencing. These include:

- Increased safety for society
- Good and prudent progression and reversal of convicts' tendencies
- Individual adaptation and tailoring
- More efficient implementation
- Freeing up prison capacity
- Freeing up resources
- Contributing to normalization in the use of technology, in line with society.

Notes

1. Verksemdsstrategi for correctional services 2021–2026 – Kriminalomsorgen.no in English: About the Norwegian Correctional Service – Kriminalomsorgen.no.
2. future-correctional services---a-joint-social mission---kdi-31.10.2019.pdf (regjeringen.no).
3. Conversation with Jan-Erik Sandlie, Deputy Head of Norwegian Correctional Services, May 20, 2022.
4. Verksemdsstrategi for correctional services 2021–2026 – Kriminalomsorgen.no in English: About the Norwegian Correctional Service – Kriminalomsorgen.no.
5. Kriminalomsorgen.no.

CLOSING REMARKS

What can others learn from Norwegian correctional services, and what led this small country in the north to pursue a more humane prison practice? We believe the answer is not black and white, but very complex. Great white papers from 1977, 1997 and 2007 have characterized the Norwegian Correctional Services over the past 50 years.

What these white papers have in common is that they have raised the discussion about what kind of correctional services we want in Norway. They have also helped to put Norway on the world map when it comes to organizing a correctional facility with a focus on rehabilitation and reducing recidivism.

The Norwegian Labor Party has been the leading and largest political party for much of this period. Early in the party's history, several of its most trusted elected representatives, such as Einar Gerhardsen and Oscar Torp, were imprisoned on political grounds. Gerhardsen's successor as prime minister, Trygve Bratteli, served, like Gerhardsen, many years in Nazi concentration camps in Germany during World War II. These people know what an inhuman prison is.

But Norway has also taken inspiration from many countries over the years. In the 1990s, Nordic Correctional Services were heavily inspired by Canada in terms of organizational and leadership development, and professional initiatives, including cognitive programs.

We adopted some of these programs, and much of the cognitive thinking is still used in programs in Norway today. In the early 1990s, there was a delegation from Norway visiting New York to see a drug-treatment program they had in their prisons there. This program was called Stayin' Out. It was adopted in Norway and still exists in several prisons under the name Stifinner'n which focuses in particular on young offenders with drug-addiction problems.

In Sweden and England, the contact arrangement for working officers simply means a closer relationship between inmate and employee.

Norwegian Correctional Services are still traveling around the world looking for inspiration and foreign prisons to collaborate with. It is always useful to look to other countries to find smarter and better solutions.

We need to be open to new ideas. For example, Poland has good payroll systems with pension schemes for inmates. In Norway, there are often complaints about the low rate of unemployment benefits for the inmates and that they lose their pension during their period in prison.

In Norwegian Correctional Services, we have put the elements that we have borrowed from others together into a whole. But the most special thing about the Norwegian model is that the relationships between inmates and staff are unique. This is the key to the success of humanistic prison care. In Norway, it is a matter of course to treat inmates with respect and humanity.

DOI: 10.4324/9781003195887-19

Nevertheless, we have no reason to be equally proud of everything concerning Norwegian prison care. Although Halden and Agder are new modern prisons, we still have many old-fashioned and impractical prison buildings. Norway has also received a lot of criticism for its isolation practices. Moreover, the sentence for women is not nearly at the same level as for men. We're not equal here yet.

In June 2019, the Parliamentary Ombudsman for Norway had to send a special message to the parliament about isolation and lack of human contact in Norwegian prisons. During the period 2014–2018, the Parliamentary Ombudsman's Prevention Unit visited 19 prisons with a high level of security. The purpose was to uncover and prevent inhumane or degrading treatment of prisoners, in line with the mandate the Parliamentary Ombudsman has been given by the UN Supplementary Protocol to the Convention on Torture. The Correctional Services have naturally responded to this criticism, and much of the challenges are related to an old and inappropriate building stock in many parts of the country. Large investments are required to correct the remarks made by the Parliamentary Ombudsman. This is possible to do, but it requires additional funding from the parliament to raise the building standard in Norwegian correctional services.[1]

Oslo Economics conducted an economic analysis of isolation-reducing measures in the Correctional Services in 2020 following criticism from the Parliamentary Ombudsman in 2019.

The conclusion of the analysis was:

> Without degrading the other achievements of the Correctional Services, it is not possible, as we see it, to achieve the community goals without investments in buildings and staffing. However, it is possible to achieve the goals at a lower cost than what KDI has estimated, if one accepts that lock-out time does not necessarily have to be accompanied by an activity offer.[2]

Another aspect of the detention that the Torture Committee has also pointed out and criticized is that the time Norwegian inmates are in custody for is often unnecessarily long. This is often due to late proceedings in the criminal-case chain – that there is a queue in the judicial system.

In the Norwegian Correctional Services' strategy, they have identified 22 forces that affect the correctional services in a long-term perspective. One of the driving forces highlighted as particularly important is "less economic room for maneuverability and a need for efficiency."

In recent years, the whole public sector in Norway has experienced economic cuts that have also affected the room for maneuverability of the Correctional Services. Not even the Correctional Services can cope without a stable and spacious financial framework, even if money is not the only thing that matters. Admittedly, some new prisons have been built, but there are several prisons that have suffered cuts in operations, and are in turn no longer of adequate service. The economic cuts year after year have also led to a reduction in the number of employees, those who are the absolute most important resource. To bring about a change in the behaviors of convicts, good and qualified staffing is required. Ideally, it should have been a one-on-one relationship, that each inmate had his or her own contact officer, but this is a lofty goal for today's Norwegian prison care.

Time is needed for good conversation, for good environmental work and to engage in dynamic security. Even in Norway we now see that this quality is challenged due to budget cuts. This is a political issue, and it has never given political parties many votes when they say they will allocate extra money to the Correctional Services.

There are at least two pillars that must be in place to call a punishment humane. One is care, and another is that there is good content that can prepare the convicted person for a crime-free existence after serving time.

It is said that the convicted person should experience seamless criminal care. This means that there should be few bureaucratic barriers during his imprisonment. The various parts of the Correctional Services shall cooperate across penal execution. The goal is that every convict should have a predictable course of punishment from the start of his sentence to the end of his sentence. The seamlessness shall contribute to promoting good individual assessments and ensure an equal punishment for convicts. The vision of the Norwegian Correctional Services today, "Punishment that changes," provides a clear direction.

Even though the Correctional Services in Norway have experienced several financial cuts, they still have a solid foundation for success in their work. The prison-officer training also provides a good platform for working with inmates and helping them change their lives. However, there are many examples of newly qualified prison officers coming out to prisons with great idealism, but quickly getting a wake-up call as they find that the map does not quite match the terrain. They simply cannot practice all the fine measures for inmates that they have learned in prison school because there are not enough financial resources in the prisons.

But what exactly makes a human being change?

If we take Trond as an example, he was a person with heavy drug problems and a 30-year criminal career.

Today he has been drug- and crime-free for over ten years. He tells us that there was a big change during his last stay in Halden Prison. Here he found an inner motivation. He thought now or never, now he had to get his life back on track. When a convict has this fundamental motivation, the Correctional Services shall facilitate the conditions so that this motivation is well preserved and contribute to the person being given the opportunities needed to "change his or her criminal pattern of action." Trond had the motivation, and Halden Prison gave him substance-abuse treatment through the substance-abuse unit and an exciting job of establishing a prison radio to be broadcast in the community on the FM band. The first of its kind in the world! He received a good progression towards his release through Halden Prison to transitional residence and later into freedom.

We must never forget that the correctional services, the prison staff, or probation officers should not change the inmates, but contribute to the inmates being motivated to change their attitude to life and learn that the best thing for everyone, both themselves and for society, is that after their release they live a crime-free life.

The purpose of Norwegian Correctional Services is not for society to take revenge on the offender as it was in the Norwegian prison services' childhood, but to contribute to the offender becoming a law-abiding individual.

This is a win-win situation, and it is a modern and humane criminal care that we would like to export to any country that wants it.

Notes

1. www.sivilombudet.no/wp-content/uploads/2019/06/SOM_Sper cent C3per cent A6rskilt-melding_WEB.pdf
2. OE Report+2020+-+Isolation Reducing+Measures.pdf

SOURCES

About Halden: Statsbyggs ferdigmelding om Halden fengsel, Statsbygg's – State Construction's – completion report in 2010 – nr 686/2010. www.statsbygg.no/files/publikasjoner/ferdigmeldinger/686_HaldenFengsel.pdf
About Isolation. www.kriminalomsorgen.no/isolasjon.535936.no.html
NOU 1984 nr. 2: Utdanning for arbeid i Kriminalomsorgen, the Norwegian Parliamentary Select Committee Report, NOU 1984:2, entitled 'Education for Employment in Correctional Services'. www.nb.no/statsmaktene/nb/d787 0b4e48569f48ab4689748d152045?lang=en&index=2#0
OsloEconomics – Analyse av ABE-reformen. www.regjeringen.no/contentassets/f0fb720d23d844879e2a5e175e42f415/analyse-av-driftssituasjonen-i-kriminalomsorgen-rev-29.05.2018.pdf
Stortingsmelding (White Paper) no. 27 (1997–98): Om Kriminalomsorgen. www.regjeringen.no/no/dokumenter/stmeld-nr-27-1998-/id191585/?ch=6
Stortingsmelding (White Paper) no. 37 (2007–08). www.regjeringen.no/contentassets/d064fb36995b4da8a23f-858c38ddb5f5/no/pdfs/stm200720080037000dddpdfs.pdf
The Civil Ombudsman's Special Report to the Parliament. www.sivilombudet.no/wp-content/uploads/2019/06/SOM_Sper cent C3per cent A6rskilt-melding_WEB.pdf

Jan Erik Sandlie, Deputy Director General in the Directorate of Norwegian Correctional Service. Board member in Euro-Pris
Harald Føsker, former director of Krus
Maria Karine Aasen-Svensrud, Parlamentarian (Labor Party)
Geir Bjørkli, *Norwegian Prison* and Probation Officers' Union
Roar Øvrebø, *Norwegian Prison* and Probation Officers' Union
Asle Aase, *Norwegian Prison* and Probation Officers' Union
Tommy Fredriksen, *Norwegian Prison* and Probation Officers' Union
Jordan Hyatt, professor Criminology and Justice Studies at Drexel University, US
Ragnar Kristoffersen, KRUS
Knut Bjarkeid, former prison governor of Ila prison
Kåre Leiksett, former top bureaucrat and central onpaper 27
Naima Khawaja, the Directorate of Norwegian Correctional Service.
Finn Dotsetsveen, former the Directorate of Norwegian Correctional Service.
Kim Ekhaugen, International director of the Directorate of Norwegian Correctional Service.
Ivar S. Jensen, Prison Officer, Bergen Prison
Rune Greve, Prison Officer, Bergen Prison
Frank Moritz Tveiten Johansen, Governor Agder fengsel

Sources

Arne Treholt, former inmate Drammen, Ila and Ullersmo
Tone Bremnes, NAV-employee working with inmates from Bredtvedt prison
Elisabeth Kjetilstad, Priest in Bredtvedt prison
Avdelingsleder Patricia Connor-Council, Chester prison
Doris Bakken, governor Bredtveit Fengsel
Randi Rosenqvist, Psykiater
Gabi Groff-Jensen, Fengselsførstebetjent/fagkoordinator NFFA Ila fengsel og forvaringsanstalt
Farukh Qureshi, Prison officer, Oslo Fengsel
Dr Marayca Lopez, Chester prison
Synnøve Andersen, professor, Universitetet i Oslo
Prison Officers Malin Anette Klund, Tina Olsen and Line Syverstad.
Autumn Engstroem, prison Officer, North Dakota
Joseph Spark, Inmate
Trond Henriksen, former inmate
Luna Vanatta, former inmate at Bredtvedt prison
Arne Treholt, former inmate in Ullersmo prison
Tommy Fredriksen, Thanks also to other who has openly shared their experience with us during the research process.

INDEX

Note: Page locators in **bold** indicate a photo

Aasen-Svensrud, Maria Karine **8**
Agder Prison 97, **98**, 99–100, 104
Amend 93
American prisons 11, 89–90, 93
Andenæs, Johs 11
Andersen, Synøve Nygaard 23, 26–27, **86**, 90
anxiety 58, 67, 78, 82
art 67–68

Bakken, Doris 68–70
bank cards 82, 99–100
Bjarkeid, Knut 14, **60**
Botsen 31
Brand, Christo xii, **xiii**, **xv**, xv–xvi
Bredtveit Prison 65–66, 70, 93

Canadian correctional services 12
cashless 98
Center for Reoffending Studies 25
Church City Mission 73
collaboration: with Amend 93; business 79; international 85
communication 50, 60, 63, 82, 99
Confederation of Trade Union (LO Norway) 4
confiscations 11, 13
Connor-Council, Patricia **86**, **88**
contact officers 15, 87
convicts: female 22; public transportation, use 1; right to education 13
cooperation 16, 50, 53, 59, 70, 77
correctional: collaborations 91, 94; service projects 94
correctional officers 41, 85
Council of Europe Torture Committee (CAT) 62
Council of Europe's Torture-Monitoring Committee (CPT) 62, 94
COVID-19 23, 87
cradle-to-grave welfare 4–5
Cramer, Victoria 58

crime 9, 16, 23, 26, 69, 81
crime-free 16, 22, 43, 104–105
criminal care 50, 79, 104–105
criminality 29, 39–40, 42
criminal reform 29

Danish Prison and Probation Service 85
depression 58, 67
detention 17, 25, 58–59, 68, 100, 104
digital visits 96
Drexel University (USA) 86
drug addiction 22, 80–81, 103
drug use 30
dynamic security 15–16, 54, 87, 91, 104

e-carceration 22
Eberhardt, Tom 93
Ekhaugen, Kim 91, 93
electronic monitoring 7, 12, **22**, 22–23, 94, 97, 100–101
Engstrøm, Autumn 93
Estenstad, Stian 75, **76**, 77–80
European court of human rights (EcHR) 61–62
Evje women's prison 65

facial recognition 101
Føsker, Harald 18–19, 30, 49–50, **51**
Fredriksen, Tommy 57

Gender Equality 66
Gerhardsen, Einar **5**, 30, 103
GPS tracking 22, 101
green prison 42–43
Groff-Jensen, Gaby 62–63

Halden Prison: architecture 41, **42**, 43; capacity 41; punishment that works 38; solar energy 43
Hammerlin, Yngve 59, 65

Index

Henriksen, Trond 1–3, 45, **46**, 46–47, 72
Høidal, Are 2, **39**, **72–73**, 74, 81, 85
home detention 11
human contact 100, 104
human mind 58
human rights 13, 19, 62, 96
Hyatt, Jordan **86**, 90–91

ideology 9, 55
Ila Prison **8**, 29, 32–35, 58–59, **60**, 62
imprisonment: forms of 16, 22, 101; network after 72, 77, 80–81
inmates: assistance 70, 83; female 21, 66–67, 70; former 75, 77–78, 81–82
interdisciplinary team 62
interfaith team 53
International Committee of the Red Cross (ICRC) 80
isolation, use of 57, 62, 96

JURK *see* women, legal advice for
justice, criminal 25, 27

Khawaja, Naima 52–53
Klund, Annette **86**
Kongsvinger Prison 65, 67
Kragerø women's prison 65–66
Kristoffersen, Ragnar 25–26
Kumla Prison 43, 85

Labor Party (Norwegian) 4, 6, 7, 9, 31, 103
Leiksett, Kåre E. **12**
little Scandinavia 85, 87; humane environment 90–91, **92**; policy revisions 88–89; teamwork 86
Lopez, Marayca 87, **88**
Lothe, Johan 81–82
Lundeby, Hilde 66

Mandela, Nelson 74, 81, 96
Mathiesen, Thomas 29
mental health challenges 13, 59, 69–70, 75, 82–83
mentally disabled 13, 58, 69
mentorship 53, 85
Minister of Justice 21, 29, 40, 101; *see also* Storberget
Mohn, George Rieber 33
Moore, Michael 38
myths 4, 33, 36, 47

National Substance Abuse Programme (NSAP) 45, 48
neo-Nazi 53–54
New European Bauhaus 42
New Halden Prison 40–41
Nilsen, Rita 81
Nordic exceptionalism 7
Nordics 4
normality, principle of 15, 17, 43, 85, 90
Norwegian: agreement with employers 5; educational system 6, 7, 13, 19, 41–42, 82; welfare system 17
Norwegian Association for Criminal Reform (KROM) 29, 59, 61

Norwegian correctional service (NCS): attention, attacks 4; principles of 13, 17, 25; rehabilitation as focus 7, 16; social mission 11, 30, 40, 47; solar energy, use of 43
Norwegian Directorate of Correctional Services 11, 52–53, 69, 93
Norwegian Foreign Service 31
Norwegian Labor and Welfare Administration (NAV) 45, 70, 78, 82–83
Norwegian National Institution for Human Rights (NIM) 62
Norwegian Prison and Probation Association (NFF) 9, 101

Olsen, Tina **86**
Ombudsman: Equality 66; Parliamentary 62, 66, 104
Oslo Penitentiary 29

Paris Agreement 42
Penal Establishment Commission 38
Penal Execution Act 52, 62, 66
penal system 15–17, 19, 29, 40
Pennsylvania Department of Corrections (PA DOC) 85, 87
Pennsylvania State Correctional Institution at Chester (SCI Chester) 85–87
permissions 30
physical punishment 28
polarization 50
Pratt, John 7
principle of proximity 9, 66
prison: conditions 9, 29, 38, 94; modern 42, 97; policy 19, 41, 57, 89, 91; population 19, 57–58, 69, 75, 91; security 15–16
Prison Act 1952/1958 30
prison boards 28, 33
prisoner: activities 100; artist work 67–68; electronic monitoring 7, 12, 22–23, 94; family reunions 87; female (*see* women); treatment of 8, 37; typical 21–22
Prison Families Alliance (PFA) 84
prison officers: competences 19–20; education of 18–19; experiences of 86; physical fitness test 19; role of 16; student 19, 30
Prison Reform Committee 28, 40
probation: officers 105; services 8, 11, 84–85, 97
professional management 79
progression 43, 54, 102, 105
psychiatric patients 29
public services 7, 13
punishment 11–12

Qureshi, Farukh 53–54, **55**

radicalization and extremism 49–50, 52–53
Radio Inside 2
Radio Prime 47, **72**, 73
Ravneberget Prison 65
recidivism rate 25–27
Red Bike project 79–80

Red Cross: help for former prisoners 77–78; partnerships 79–80; volunteers 76
Reform Committee 19, 28–29, 40
rehabilitation, focus on 9, 11–12, 38, 62, **73**, 87, 91, 103
relapse 9, 12, 25
release 26, 29–30, 70, 75
re-offending 23, 25, 27
research 25–26, 65
retreat 43
Retretten 80
Return Center 79
Ringerike Prison 85
Rolling Stones 1
Romerike Prison 62, 68, 85
Rosenqvist, Randi 14, 57–61

Salvation Army 83
Sanders, Bernie 6
Sandlie, Jan Erik **12**
Sarpsborg Prison 29, 40–41
Scandinavian Penal History, Culture and Prison Practice (Scarff Smith) 9
Scarff Smith, Peter 9
Sentences Act 22
sexual abuse 67, 97, 100
silence and tranquility 44
Skardhamar, Torbjørn 26–27
social democracy 7
Solheim, Ingrid E. 65
solitary confinement 33, 35, 46, 50, 61
Spinks, Joe 91. **92**
Statistics Norway (SSB) 21–22, 60
Storberget, Knut: Minister of Justice 2, 12, 26, **39**, 46, 50
Strømme, Dan 66
substance-abuse: care 59, 82; problem 45–46, 59; unit 2, 45, **46**, 47, 105

suicide 58–60
swastikas 53–54
Swedish Prison and Probation Service 85
Syverstad, Line 85, **86**

Telle, Kjetil 23
terror attacks 49–50
trade-union movement 9–10
traffic offenders 23, 27, 101
Treholt, Arne 31, **32**, 33–37
Trond: enters prison 1; second chance 47
Tveiten Johansen, Frank M. 98

Ugelvik, Thomas 9
Ullersmo Prison 3, 31, 35–36, 62, 68
UN Torture Committee (CCPR) 62
unemployment 6, 9, 103
University College of Norwegian Correctional Service (KRUS) 19–20, 25, 30, 68, 93
University of Oslo (Norway) 26, 29, 86

Valle, Inger Louise 21, 40
Vanatta, Luna **67**, 67–68
Viking blood 75
Vikings 4, 93

Way Back 81–82
welfare policies 9
Wetzel, John 85
White Papers 12, 40, 103
Williams, Brie 93
women: legal advice for 66; in prison, conditions 65, 66–38
Women's Reconciliation Committee 65
worldview team 53
World War II 5, 30, 50, 65, 103

Zelentsov, Yury 83–84